Attention-Deficit/ Hyperactivity Disorder

Attention-Deficit/Hyperactivity Disorder

Autism

Blindness and Vision Impairment

Brain Injury

Chronic Illness

Deaf and Hard of Hearing

Emotional Disturbance

Gender Issues

Intellectual Disabilities

Learning Disabilities

Physical Challenges

Protective Services

Speech Impairment

The Foster Care System

The Juvenile Court System

The Laws That Protect Youth with Special Needs

Attention-Deficit/ Hyperactivity Disorder

SHIRLEY BRINKERHOFF

MASON CREST

Mason Crest
450 Parkway Drive, Suite D
Broomall, PA 19008
www.masoncrest.com

Printed and bound in the United States of America.

Series ISBN: 978-1-4222-3027-5
ISBN: 978-1-4222-3028-2
ebook ISBN: 978-1-4222-8813-9

Library of Congress Cataloging-in-Publication Data

Brinkerhoff, Shirley.
  Attention-deficit/hyperactivity disorder / Shirley Brinkerhoff.
    pages cm. — (Living with a special need.)
  Includes index.
  Audience: Grade 7-8
  ISBN 978-1-4222-3028-2 (hardback) — ISBN 978-1-4222-3027-5 (series) — ISBN
978-1-4222-8813-9 (ebook) 1. Attention-deficit hyperactivity disorder—Juvenile
literature I. Title.
  RJ506.H9B754 2014
  618.92'8589—dc23
                          2014010618

Picture credits: Andrea Danti - Fotolia.com: p. 83; Artville: p. 35; Benjamin Stewart:
pp. 51, 115; Digital Vision: p. 37; Life Art: pp. 38, 41; Photo Alto: pp. 18, 19, 22, 71,
86, 88; PhotoDisc: pp. 17, 23, 33, 34, 40, 42, 53, 54, 64, 65, 66, 69, 72, 81, 84, 96,
104, 107, 117. Individuals portrayed in these images are models, and the images are in-
tended for illustrative purposes only.

CONTENTS

KEY ICONS TO LOOK FOR:

Text-Dependent Questions: These questions send the reader back to the text for more careful attention to the evidence presented there.

Words to Understand: These words with their easy-to-understand definitions will increase the reader's understanding of the text, while building vocabulary skills.

Series Glossary of Key Terms: This back-of-the book glossary contains terminology used throughout this series. Words found here increase the reader's ability to read and comprehend higher-level books and articles in this field.

Research Projects: Readers are pointed toward areas of further inquiry connected to each chapter. Suggestions are provided for projects that encourage deeper research and analysis.

Sidebars: This boxed material within the main text allows readers to build knowledge, gain insights, explore possibilities, and broaden their perspectives by weaving together additional information to provide realistic and holistic perspectives.

A child with special needs is not defined by his disability.
It is just one part of who he is.

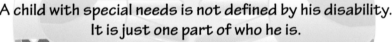

INTRODUCTION

Each child is unique and wonderful. And some children have differences we call special needs. Special needs can mean many things. Sometimes children will learn differently, or hear with an aid, or read with Braille. A young person may have a hard time communicating or paying attention. A child can be born with a special need, or acquire it by an accident or through a health condition. Sometimes a child will be developing in a typical manner and then become delayed in that development. But whatever problems a child may have with her learning, emotions, behavior, or physical body, she is always a person first. She is not defined by her disability; instead, the disability is just one part of who she is.

Inclusion means that young people with and without special needs are together in the same settings. They learn together in school; they play together in their communities; they all have the same opportunities to belong. Children learn so much from each other. A child with a hearing impairment, for example, can teach another child a new way to communicate using sign language. Someone else who has a physical disability affecting his legs can show his friends how to play wheelchair basketball. Children with and without special needs can teach each other how to appreciate and celebrate their differences. They can also help each other discover how people are more alike than they are different. Understanding and appreciating how we all have similar needs helps us learn empathy and sensitivity.

In this series, you will read about young people with special needs from the unique perspectives of children and adolescents who are experiencing the disability firsthand. Of course, not all children with a particular disability are the same as the characters in the stories. But the stories demonstrate at an emotional level how a special need impacts a child, his family, and his friends. The factual material in each chapter will expand your horizons by adding to your knowledge about a particular disability. The series as a whole will help you understand differences better and appreciate how they make us all stronger and better.

—*Cindy Croft*
Educational Consultant

YOUTH WITH SPECIAL NEEDS provides a unique forum for demystifying a wide variety of childhood medical and developmental disabilities. Written to captivate an adolescent audience, the books bring to life the challenges and triumphs experienced by children with common chronic conditions such as hearing loss, mental retardation, physical differences, and speech difficulties. The topics are addressed frankly through a blend of fiction and fact. Students and teachers alike can move beyond the information provided by accessing the resources offered at the end of each text.

This series is particularly important today as the number of children with special needs is on the rise. Over the last two decades, advances in pediatric medical techniques have allowed children who have chronic illnesses and disabilities to live longer, more functional lives. As a result, these children represent an increasingly visible part of North American population in all aspects of daily life. Students are exposed to peers with special needs in their classrooms, through extracurricular activities, and in the community. Often, young people have misperceptions and unanswered questions about a child's disabilities—and more important, his or her *abilities*. Many times, there is no vehicle for talking about these complex issues in a comfortable manner.

This series provides basic information that will leave readers with a deeper understanding of each condition, along with an awareness of some of the associated emotional impacts on affected children, their families, and their peers. It will also encourage further conversation about these issues. Most important, the series promotes a greater comfort for its readers as they live, play, and work side by side with these individuals who have medical and developmental differences—youth with special needs.

—Dr. Lisa Albers, Dr. Carolyn Bridgemohan, Dr. Laurie Glader
Medical Consultants

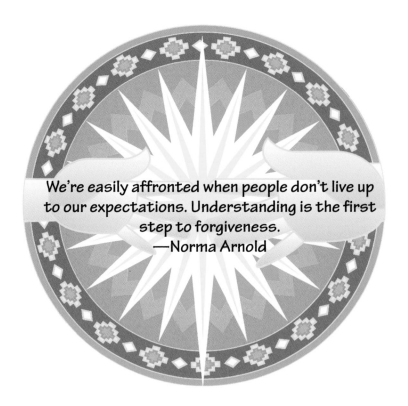

We're easily affronted when people don't live up to our expectations. Understanding is the first step to forgiveness.
—Norma Arnold

Words to Understand

hyperactivity: Extremely, and in some cases abnormally, active.

impulsivity: The condition of acting or being likely to act suddenly, without forethought.

ADHD/inattentive type: Attention-deficit/hyperactivity disorder characterized by the difficulty in paying attention and staying on task.

aversive: Producing a definite dislike for or feeling against something.

ADHD/hyperactivity-impulsivity: Attention-deficit/hyperactivity disorder characterized by inappropriate physical activity.

cognitive: The process of knowing, which includes perception, memory, and judgment.

1

GETTING TO KNOW CONNOR

I guess I should have known Connor was different right from the first day we brought him home. He screamed his head off the whole time I was trying to introduce myself, and he kept sucking his skinny red fists so hard I was afraid he'd suck the bracelet right over his hand.

I didn't have a lot of experience with babies back then, so I didn't know what to look for. I mean, up till then I'd *been* the baby. So how was I supposed to spot the danger signals?

There probably ought to be a handbook for big sisters with a title like *The Ten Most Important Signs That You Have a Brother with ADHD, and What to Do About It.* Since there isn't a book, maybe this journal will help me understand what is happening.

It didn't take me long to catch on, though. My two older brothers had a room to themselves, and of course my parents did, too. Since there were only three bedrooms in our house, you can probably guess who got to share her room with the new baby, right? Right.

I was only seven that year, so when I complained about Connor keeping me awake all night with his crying, my parents said it was a good thing he was sharing *my* room. "Since first-graders still get a rest time after lunch, you can take a nap if you need to," they said. "Your big brothers have to stay awake all day for their classes."

I pointed out to them that sleep deprivation can stunt your growth and that, at the rate Connor was keeping me awake, I might end up being the shortest big sister in the world. They just laughed and told my oldest brother Kevin to stop teaching me to say things like "sleep deprivation."

We all learned to put up with Connor over the next few years. My parents enclosed the screened-in porch and made it into a bedroom for Connor, so I eventually got to sleep through the night again. That was one big problem solved. But he still spent a lot of time making noise and messing up the house.

And he always struck when you least expected it. Like the day my big brothers, Kevin and Tim, and I spent an hour building a waist-high Lincoln Log fort in Kevin's bedroom. The plan was that when we finished, Kevin would give Tim a signal, and Tim would switch on this video we have about the Battle of the Alamo. It has all these great battle noises in the soundtrack, and we were supposed to reenact the battle around the Lincoln Log fort. What we didn't know was that Connor was crouched just outside Kevin's bedroom doorway, listening. Just as I carefully put the very last Lincoln Log in place, Kevin shouted to Tim, "Okay, hit it!" Connor, who takes everything literally, did just that. He jumped into the room and hit the fort with all his might. Lincoln Logs flew everywhere, and we all chased after Connor, yelling what we were going to do to him when we caught him. But Connor is just about the fastest person you'll ever meet, and catching him is almost impossible—even for my big brothers.

Then there was the time Connor decided to take apart my new jewelry box—the musical one that you wound up and the ballerina danced around and around to "Somewhere, My Love." He said he "just wanted to find out how it worked." Except it never worked again after that, of course.

Nobody in our family will ever forget the day Connor decided to play "mailman." He went to every house on our street and took the neighbors' mail out of their mailboxes and dumped it all into his wagon. Then he "delivered" the mail himself, putting a few pieces back into each mailbox. Of course, he couldn't read back then, so you can imagine what our neighbors found when they went to get their mail.

But sometimes—I have to admit—Connor could be very sweet. Just when you thought you couldn't stand one more minute of having him around, he'd snuggle up to you with that freckly face and those round blue eyes and say something like, "I lub you, Shauna."

So, you can see there wasn't too much trouble with Connor before he started to school, if you don't count the little things, like the time he tried to mow the lawn with my dad's new riding mower (he ruined the engine when he poured oil in the gas tank); or the time he dressed up like Santa Claus and tried to go down the chimney of our backyard brick barbeque (he got stuck and the fire department had to come and pull him out); or the experiment he conducted on our beagle Cuddles to see if he liked Tabasco sauce on his dog food.

The *real* trouble didn't start until Connor was five and my parents had to let him out of the house on a regular basis. I was twelve and working hard on being a normal member of the sixth grade. The way to do this, as everybody knows, is to NOT STAND OUT in any way. Like, you don't want to look different, or talk different, or wear weird clothes, or get really, really good grades or really, really bad grades—stuff like that.

Most of all, you don't want to have family members who are different. (Or if you do, you never let the other sixth-graders find out about it.) So when Connor began kindergarten and his reputation started getting around at Conwell Consolidated School, where all four of us O'Leary kids were students at the same time, I knew my standing as a normal sixth-grader was in trouble—big, big trouble, because Connor was a member of my family. And if he was anything, he was definitely *different*.

The notes started coming home with Connor from his very first day of kindergarten. The bright orange notes from Conwell Consolidated have all these pre-printed descriptions of bad stuff students can do. That way, parents can see at a glance what their kids did wrong that day. Beside each printed description is an empty box, so teachers don't have to waste any effort and actually write words. All they have to do is check the box beside the right description: "Does not play well with others," "Is disruptive in class," "Does not show proper respect for the possessions of others"—you get the idea.

The last box on the note is the clincher, the one that we all hope and pray our teachers never check: "Teacher requests conference with parents."

By the time Connor was in kindergarten, our oldest brother Kevin was fifteen and in the tenth grade, and Tim was in eighth, so my parents were pretty old, I guess, but not old enough to have that much gray hair. Not old enough to look that tired, either, but they did. And every day that Connor brought home another note—which was most days—they looked a little grayer and a little tireder.

Meanwhile, I had my own problems. Since I was working so hard on being a normal sixth-grader, like I already explained, it was necessary for me to ignore Connor when I saw him in the hall at school or on the playground. I explained this all to him at home the night before his first day of school. (This may sound mean, but I swear I did it in the nicest possible way.)

"Look, Connor," I told him while we walked Cuddles to the park, "I know you're my brother. And you're a pretty good one, too," I added, so he wouldn't feel bad or anything. "But when we're at school, it would be better if people didn't know we're related. So don't talk to me there, okay?"

Connor didn't say anything, for once.

I tried again. "You know, like where you see me in the hall, Connor. Or when we're on the playground."

"Why?" he asked.

I thought for a minute. "I can't explain that; it'd be too hard for you to understand."

"But lots of people already know I'm your brother!" he said.

"Right. But we don't want to remind them about that too often, you know? Like, if we don't talk while we're at school, maybe they won't make a big deal of it. So just don't talk to me when you see me, okay?"

"But what if I need you, Shauna?"

I could see I would never make any headway like this. I tried again. "You won't *need* me, Connor. The teachers take care of you when you're in kindergarten." Then I had a brilliant idea. "Listen, how about we work out a little deal: I'll give you two Pokemon cards for every day you don't talk to me at school, okay?"

"All right!" he yelled.

I felt a little bad about that, I admit. I haven't cared about my Pokemon cards since about the time Connor was born, but he didn't have to know that. I just figured I was creating what my dad called a "win-win" situation—I won the chance to be a normal sixth-grader, and Connor won all those Pokemon cards he's so crazy about. I was pretty pleased with myself for working things out so well.

Except, since Connor was involved, things didn't work out so well after all.

DEFINING ADHD

According to the DSM-5 (the *Diagnostic and Statistical Manual of Mental Disorders*, the most recent classification of mental disorders by the American Psychiatric Association), the essential feature of attention-deficit/hyperactivity disorder (ADHD) is "a persistent pattern of inattention and/or **hyperactivity** and **impulsivity** that is more frequently displayed and more severe than is typically observed in individuals at a comparable level of development."

Other features include:

- some hyperactive-impulsive or inattentive symptoms causing impairment before the age of twelve
- impairment from the symptoms must be present in at least two places, such as home, school, or work
- symptoms must show evidence of interfering with developmentally appropriate functioning at school, work, or during social occasions
- must not occur exclusively during the course of schizophrenia or another psychotic disorder and must not be better explained by another mental disorder, such as a depressive or bipolar disorder, anxiety disorder, dissociative disorder, personality disorder, or substance intoxication or withdrawal.

If six or more symptoms are displayed often for a period of at least six months from either *inattentive type* ADHD or hyperactivity-impulsivity categories (as described on the following pages), the child can be diagnosed as having ADHD.

Inattentive-Type ADHD

- failing to pay attention to details; making careless mistakes at work or school
- doing messy work; work done carelessly, without considered thought; difficulty sustaining attention and completing tasks
- frequently appearing as if one's mind is somewhere else; as if one either is not listening or did not hear

A child with ADHD may act silly when important conversations are taking place.

- frequent shifts between unfinished activities; lack of follow-through on schoolwork, chores, or other duties
- difficulty organizing tasks and activities
- seeing tasks requiring sustained mental effort, organizational demands, or close concentration as *aversive*
- work habits that are frequently disorganized; materials for the task are often scattered, lost, carelessly handled, or damaged
- being easily distracted by trivial noises or events or irrelevant stimuli
- forgetfulness about daily activities, such as forgetting school lunches or missing appointments
- inattention in conversation, including frequent shifts, not listening, not focusing on the conversation, or not following rules of games

Children with ADHD may kick their feet and fidget frequently in the classroom.

A child with ADHD may want to be active all the time.

Hyperactivity-Impulsivity

- fidgetiness or squirming
- not remaining seated when appropriate
- excessive running or climbing in inappropriate situations
- difficulty playing or engaging quietly in leisure activities
- difficulty waiting for one's turn; interrupting; blurting out answers inappropriately
- actions that may lead to accidents; engaging in potentially dangerous activities without considering possible consequences

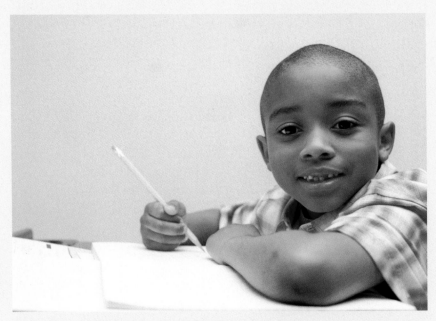

Not every child who has problems concentrating in school has ADHD.

Make Connections: Learning Disabilities & ADHD

Many children who have ADHD also have a learning disorder. Although the studies vary, 25 to 70 percent of children with ADHD have a learning disability, and from 15 to 35 percent of children with a learning disability have ADHD. This is because attention and learning are related brain processes. "Learning" requires attention—and it's hard to give your attention to something you can't understand! This is why these disorders often go hand-in-hand.

The average age for diagnosis of ADHD is between six and eight years of age. It is important to note that not all extremely active babies will later be diagnosed with this disorder. For ADHD to be diagnosed, the behaviors must, however, appear early in life (before age twelve), and continue for at least six months. The behaviors must be more frequent or severe than the behaviors of others the same age. Most important, the behaviors must create a real handicap in at least two areas of a person's life, such as school, home, work, or social settings. In other words, if a child's schoolwork or friendships were not affected by these behaviors, he would not be diagnosed with ADHD—and if a child has problems at school but nowhere else, she wouldn't be diagnosed as having ADHD either.

PAYING ATTENTION

When people with ADHD have to pay attention to things they find dull, they often create their own excitement. They may dream about action heroes and come up with new exciting plots, including scary monsters or powerful weapons.

They may become so interested in developing new adventures or sketching new weapons that an entire class goes by at school without them hearing a word the teacher says.

People with ADHD may perceive the world from a different perspective.

Many children with ADHD have another learning disorder as well.

Research Project

The Diagnostic and Statistical Manual of Mental Disorders (DSM) is sometimes called the "bible" for professionals who work in special education and mental health. It creates the definition for every condition, so that professionals can use a single standard when they're working with people who have these conditions.

Go online to find out more about this book. When was it first written? Who writes it? How often is it updated? Does everyone agree that it should be used as the standard? Why or why not?

HOW COMMON IS ADHD?

According to the National Institute of Mental Health, between 3 and 5 percent of kindergarten and school-age children are affected by ADHD, which means that on average, at least one child in each classroom is likely to be have this condition.

Boys are more likely to have ADHD than girls are. One study found that about two to three times as many boys as girls are diagnosed with ADHD. ADHD always begins in

When a child with ADHD is bored, she may use her imagination to create her own interior excitement. Unfortunately, this usually means she misses what is going on around her in school.

Text-Dependent Questions

1. List the symptoms of ADHD that you see in Connor's behavior in this chapter.
2. How old are most children when they are diagnosed with ADHD?
3. If a child's behavior is wild and uncontrolled at school, but she sits quietly and pays attention to what others are saying when she's with her family, would she be diagnosed with ADHD? Why or why not?
4. How are learning disabilities and ADHD related?

childhood (whether or not it is recognized), but it often lasts into adulthood. According to several recent studies, between 30 and 65 percent of children with ADHD will still have symptoms when they are teenagers and adults.

If one is ashamed, there is no better remedy than to practice kindness.
—Mencius

Words to Understand

labeling: Applying a word or phrase to someone as a convenient, generalized classification.

dehumanize: To deprive of human qualities; to make inhuman or machinelike.

imply: To suggest or hint at something.

proponents: People in favor of something.

genetic: Having to do with material that is passed from generation to generation through the genes.

megavitamin: A large quantity of vitamins.

toxins: Poisons.

nicotine: The main chemical in tobacco (which is poisonous).

2

EMBARRASSMENT

Connor's biggest problem is that he's always thinking about things that have nothing to do with anything that matters—lots of things and all at the same time—instead of paying attention to what he's supposed to be working on.

"Pay attention to me, Connor," I've heard Mom tell him that about a zillion times. She even gets down on her knees in the middle of the kitchen floor so she can be on his eye level. Then she puts one hand on either side of his face real gently and says, "Look me in the eyes while I talk, Honey. That way I know you're paying attention." When he looks into her eyes, she says whatever it is she wants him to hear, v-e-r-y s-l-o-w-l-y, and then makes him repeat it back to her. Once she's relatively sure he's got the idea, she lets go of his face. In the blink of an eye, Connor's gone like the wind.

And ninety-nine times out of a hundred, so is the idea.

Later on, when she asks him why he didn't set the table, or make his bed, or do whatever job she gave him during their eye-to-eye discussion, Connor always stands there looking like a deer caught in the headlights and says, "I forgot." When she asks him what he was thinking about while she was talking, it usually turns out to be something totally wild, like the time he said he was trying to figure out how to throw a web from his upstairs bedroom window to the maple tree beside our swimming pool. "Just like Spiderman, Mom! Then I could crawl out my window to the tree and dive right into the pool. Wouldn't that be cool?"

27

See what I mean? He's always thinking about stuff that has nothing to do with what he's supposed to be working on.

During Connor's first week of school, I was pretty satisfied that none of my friends recognized him. He had this new haircut—real short all over, with the hairs in front gelled to stand up stiff like the bristles of a hairbrush, so he didn't look much like the way he usually looks. Besides, I think a lot of my friends had forgotten I had a little brother—I hardly ever invited them over to my house anymore because I didn't want them to see Connor in action. I usually worked it out to get invited to *their* houses, instead. And I never mentioned him when I was there.

It was all part of my plan. And it worked pretty well at first, since most of my friends were far more interested in the brothers at the other end of my family—Kevin, who was now on the football team, and Tim, who was getting to be quite the hockey star, even though he was only in eighth grade.

That first week of kindergarten, those bright orange Conwell Consolidated notes from the teacher appeared in Connor's backpack four times.

"Does not play well with others" was checked on Monday.

"Does not show proper respect for the possessions of others" was checked on Tuesday.

"Is disruptive in class" took first place by getting checked on both Wednesday and Thursday.

On Thursday evening, Mom and Dad took Connor into his bedroom, shut the door, and had a *very* long discussion with him. There was no orange note on Friday.

At school, I saw Connor across the lunchroom every day, but I always looked the other way, scared he'd forget our deal and talk to me or try to trade his banana for my Twinkies or something.

On Wednesday, at recess, I had a close call. Connor was acting even crazier than usual, jetting around the playground like a wild man, running into other kindergartners and knocking them over right and left. Leah stopped playing, right in the middle of kickball, and stared at him with squinted eyes. "Hey, Shauna," she asked me, "isn't that your—"

I grabbed the kickball and ran. Better to get her mad at me for stealing the ball than remind her about my brother!

Every day, Connor turned up at my bedroom door after school, hand outstretched. And every day, I pulled two "common" cards from my Pokemon deck and gave them to him. On Friday, in honor of the fact that he didn't bring home an orange note, I broke down and handed him an "uncommon" and a "rare." I thought he'd be excited to get them, but I was wrong. He didn't even say thank you, just took them silently and started to walk away.

"Hey, you're not even grateful that I gave you two of my best cards?" I asked him, hands on my hips.

Connor shrugged. "I'd rather have a sister who likes me," he said, and left me standing there with my mouth hanging open.

On Monday, the orange notes started up again. I guess you can tell you're in serious trouble when the teacher takes time to write *words* on the note, besides checking boxes. I saw Monday's note for myself because Mom and Dad forgot and left it on the kitchen counter when they took Connor into his bedroom for another private talk session.

"Does not play well with others" had a big, black checkmark beside it, again. This time, though, there was also a handwritten note at the bottom, in picture-perfect teacher cursive: *Connor is creating a problem by sneezing into Lily's hair throughout the day. This behavior must stop immediately!*

Uh-oh, I thought. Mrs. Graham, the kindergarten teacher, must really be ticked.

Lily is the tiniest person in Connor's class. She's shorter than the other kindergartners, and she's so thin he could probably blow her away if he sneezed too hard. Absolutely the only thing big about Lily is her bright-red, naturally curly hair. (You can tell it's natural, because nobody would make her hair that curly on purpose.) It hangs all the way down to her waist, and it's just one big bush of red curls, puffed way out from her head on both sides and in the back.

I leaned against the kitchen counter, gnawing on my Granny Smith apple and trying to picture my little brother sneezing into that wild, red cloud of hair. You can see why it made me laugh.

On Tuesday's orange note, the same square was checked. This time, the cursive writing read, *"Today, Connor managed to get four gluesticks stuck in Lily's hair. Please call me tonight!"* "Tonight" had thick, double black lines drawn beneath it.

I knew I shouldn't be nosy, but this time I couldn't resist. When Connor came to my door later for his Pokemon cards, I said, "So, Connor, I hear you're causing a little problem with Lily."

He grabbed at the cards, but I held them just out of his reach.

"Am not," he said.

"Right!" I said. "Then why did Mrs. Graham say you were sneezing in her hair? And sticking glue sticks in it?"

He jumped as high as he could, trying to snatch the cards. "Because I have to sit right beside her at our table, and whenever she leans over to color, her dumb hair spreads everywhere, even in my face. It tickled my nose and it made me sneeze. Her hair got stuff in it when I sneezed, but I couldn't help it."

"Oh, gross!" I told him. "And how do you explain the four glue sticks?"

Connor looked uncomfortable and seemed to forget about the Pokemon cards for a second. "I was just trying to figure something out," he mumbled.

"Like how to cause more trouble in one day than you ever have before?"

He started talking really fast then, the way he does when he gets upset. "I was not either trying to cause trouble! When Lily put her head down on the table at rest time, her dumb hair went all over my stuff again. Can I help it that my glue stick was open and got tangled up in it? And then—" His voice dropped to almost a whisper. "When I saw it there, I just wondered how many more I could get to stick in her hair before she noticed. So I kind of—

borrowed—glue sticks from the other kids at my table and stuck them to her hair, that's all! I was doing an experiment, like Tim's doing with his frogs."

"Let me get this straight," I said. "You're comparing the biology experiment Tim and his friends have been working on over the entire summer—the one they caught fifty-seven frogs for—to stealing glue sticks and putting them in a little girl's hair?"

"Yeah." Connor's voice sounded so desperate that I looked at him closer. I could've sworn he had tears in his eyes. I handed him the Pokemon cards, and he stuffed them in his pocket fast, like he was afraid I'd change my mind.

I wanted to say something nice to him then, but when I opened my mouth, all that came out was, "Try not to completely destroy our family's reputation, okay, bud?" At first I felt bad, then I remembered that I had to stay tough here. What mattered was making sure that people in the sixth grade, and the rest of the school for that matter, did not associate me with this crazy kid.

And all in all, I thought we were doing pretty well with my keep-Connor-secret program. Until the next day.

That was Wednesday, and right at the beginning of the sixth grade lunch period, before any kindergartners were even supposed to be in the lunchroom, Connor shot through the doorway and straight across the room toward the table where I was eating lunch with Leah and my other friends.

"Shauna! Shauna!" he yelled, tears pouring down both cheeks. "Help me! She's gonna kill me when she finds out, Shauna!" He threw his arms around my neck and held on with all his might.

I closed my eyes and groaned.

Make Connections:
Labeling—A Dangerous Business

All children are far more than any disabilities they may have. Suppose you have asthma, for example. Having asthma is just one part of who you are. You wouldn't want people to call you "the asthmatic kid" every time they referred to you! The same is true for kids with ADHD. Labeling children ignores the characteristics that make each one a unique individual. It also can discourage children from rising above their difficulties because it can imply that they will never be able to find ways to live successfully with their challenges.

WHAT CAUSES ADHD?

No one knows for sure yet what causes ADHD, although there are many theories. Medical experts don't know if there is a single cause, or if several factors combine to cause ADHD and related learning disabilities.

The Brain Damage Theory

Researchers once speculated that attention disorders and learning disabilities were caused by minor head injuries or undetectable damage to the brain from early infections or complications at birth. Based on this theory, both attention disorders and learning disabilities were once called "minimal brain damage" or "minimal brain dysfunction." Certain types of head injury *can* explain some cases of attention disorder, but this theory could explain only a very small number of cases, and it is no longer accepted.

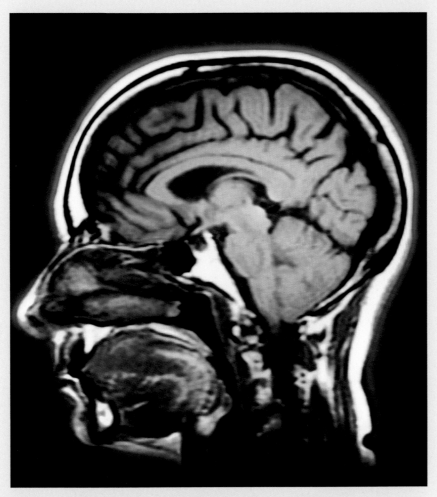

Certain types of injury to the brain can cause ADHD. These may show up on an MRI image like that shown here.

The Food Additive Theory

Another theory researchers have offered as a cause for ADHD was that refined sugar and food additives make children hyperactive and inattentive. **Proponents** of this theory encouraged parents to stop serving children foods containing artificial flavorings, preservatives, and sugars.

However, this theory has also come under question. In 1982, the National Institutes of Health (NIH), the federal agency responsible for biomedical research, held a major scientific conference to discuss the issue. After studying the data, the scientists concluded that the restricted diet only

Some people believe that eating natural foods that contain no artificial additives may help children with ADHD. However, the research has not backed up this theory.

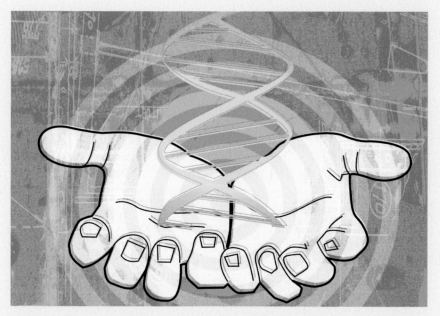

ADHD may have a genetic link.

seemed to help about 5 percent of children with ADHD, mostly either young children or children with food allergies.

The Nutritional Theory

In recent years there has been an increasing focus on the role of diet in ADHD. Some studies have found that children's symptoms may improve when they take daily vitamin and mineral supplements. But scientific studies have not yet proved this.

Scientists have reported that certain dietary factors may impact any child's behavior, including omega-3 fatty acids, found in oily fish (such as salmon, herring, mackerel, anchovies and sardines), flaxseeds, and linseeds. However, there is no proof that lacking these fatty acids actually causes ADHD. Instead, scientists think that diet can affect behavior and learning in all children, not just children with ADHD.

Research has also been conducted on iron and zinc. Iron deficiency is found in some children with ADHD. It is vital for brain function and individuals with iron-deficiency anemia can experience apathy, depression and fatigue, but tests of supplements have so far not proven anything definite.

Megavitamin therapy and various herbal supplements have also been investigated. One of the earliest diets for treating ADHD, the Feingold Diet, was developed in the early 1970s by the director of an allergy clinic in California. Benjamin Feingold connected hyperactive behavior to foods containing salicylates (chemical substances used for reducing pain, such as aspirin) and dyes. His diet restricted fruits that were considered salicylate ash foods, as well as all foods that contained artificial dyes and colors, which included lunch meats, cereals, manufactured baked goods, soft drinks and drink mixes, and manufactured candies, as well as pediatric medicines, toothpastes, and mouthwashes, among other things.

Not everyone accepts these theories, however. Today, most researchers believe that ADHD is not caused by:

- too much TV
- food allergies
- too much sugar
- poor home life
- poor schools

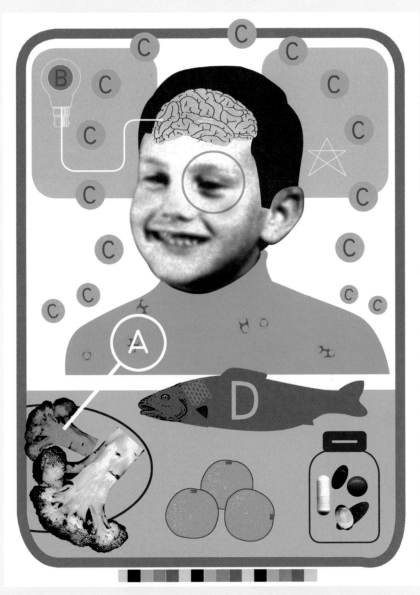

Hopeful parents look to diet and vitamin therapy to help their children with ADHD.

Brain Activity

In recent years, as new tools and techniques for studying the brain have been developed, scientists have been able to test more theories about what causes ADHD. Using one such technique, scientists demonstrated a link between a person's ability to pay attention and the level of activity in the brain. The investigators found important differences between people who have ADHD and those who don't. Brain imaging studies have revealed that the brains of children with ADHD mature normally, but that they are delayed, on average, by about three years. The delay is most pronounced in brain regions involved in thinking, paying attention, and planning. More recent studies have found that the outermost layer of the brain, the cortex, shows delayed

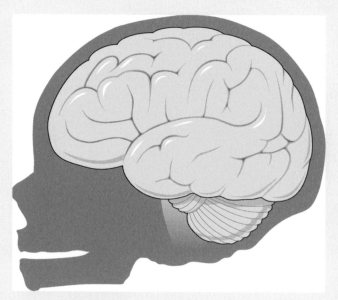

The secret to ADHD's cause and cure lies inside the brain.

maturation overall. Another brain structure important for proper communications between the two halves of the brain also shows an abnormal growth pattern. These delays and abnormalities may help to explain the patterns of behavior shown by people with ADHD.

For years, researchers assumed that ADHD was caused by an inability in the brain to filter out competing inputs; in other words, a child with this problem would be constantly distracted by sights and sounds because of neurological impairment. However, more recent research indicates that ADHD is not a disorder of attention so much as it is a developmental failure in the brain circuitry that underlies inhibition and self-control. This means that children with ADHD cannot control their responses to sensory input. Other researchers have found that these children are less capable of thinking ahead, preparing their actions in anticipation of upcoming events. They also fail to slow down to improve their accuracy at a task, even though they have been given feedback that they are making mistakes.

Scientists still don't know why the brains of children with ADHD develop more slowly, but mutations in several genes may play a role. Some of these mutations may be caused by drug use during pregnancy, **toxins**, and genetics.

Research shows that a mother's use of cigarettes, alcohol, or other drugs during pregnancy may damage the unborn child, particularly the fetus's brain. Alcohol and **nicotine** may damage nerve cells as they develop. For example, heavy alcohol use during pregnancy has been linked to fetal alcohol syndrome (FAS), a condition that can lead to low birth weight, intellectual impairment, and certain physical defects. Many children born with FAS show much the same hyperactivity, inattention, and impulsivity as children with ADHD. Drugs such as cocaine also affect the normal development

of the brain by damaging the brain-cell parts that help transmit incoming signals from our skin, eyes, and ears, and help control our responses to the environment. Current research suggests that such damage may lead to ADHD.

Toxins in the environment may also disrupt brain development or brain processes. Lead, for example, is found in dust, soil, some water pipes, and flaking paint in areas where leaded gasoline and paint were once used. Children exposed to lead may develop symptoms associated with ADHD, but only a few cases have actually been documented.

Premature births, alcohol and tobacco use by mothers during pregnancy, exposure to high levels of lead during early childhood, and brain injuries may in fact cause some cases of ADHD—but together, these factors explain only 20 to 30 percent of ADHD cases among boys, and an even smaller percentage among girls. Most cases of ADHD are linked to genetic inheritance.

Research Project

Scientists study twins to understand how genetics might influence ADHD—but they also study twins to investigate many other conditions. Go online and do a search for "twin studies." See if you can find the answers to these questions:

- How do identical twins develop after conception? What does this mean in terms of their genetic makeup?
- How long have researchers been interested in twins?
- What does phrase "nurture versus nature" mean? What does it have to do with twin studies?

Genetic Causes

The most conclusive evidence that genetics play a role in ADHD comes from studies of twins. One research study indicates that between 55 and 92 percent of the identical twins of children with ADHD will eventually develop the condition as well. Another large study of twins found that ADHD has a heritability of close to 80 percent. In other words, up to 80 percent of the differences in attention, hyperactivity, and impulsivity between people with ADHD and those without can be explained by genetic factors.

By studying twins, scientists can learn more about the role that genetics plays in ADHD.

Text-Dependent Questions

1. Describe the five possible causes of ADHD.
2. How do the brains of children with ADHD differ from the brains of other children?
3. Explain why twins are important to scientists' understanding of ADHD's genetic causes.

Researchers believe that the defective genes are the ones that tell dopamine, a chemical in the brain, how to carry messages from one nerve cell to another. This means that the children who have these genes will have less control over their own behavior.

Intolerance is blind . . . and destructive.
—Susanna Percy

3

DISASTER

I could feel my face turn bright red—okay, purple, if I'm honest—while Leah and the others at my table just kept staring at me. I tried over and over to pry Connor's arms off my neck, but he held on like a boa constrictor, crying, "Help me, Shauna! I didn't mean to do it! Don't let her get me!"

I glanced around the table and saw my chance to be a normal sixth-grader going down the drain forever. I stood up, with Connor's arms still wrapped around my neck, and carried him to the hall where we could talk.

"What are you doing, Connor?" I snapped at him in the empty hallway. "You're not even supposed to be at lunch yet!" I tugged at his arms with all my might, and this time he slid to the floor in front of me.

"I got in trouble, Shauna, and I knew you'd be in the lunchroom so I just ran to find you, and you have to help me hide!"

At the same moment, we both saw his teacher, Mrs. Graham, come barreling around the corner of the gym, heading right at us. Connor threw his skinny arms around my waist and buried his face against my sweater.

"Quick! Tell me what you did before she gets here," I ordered him.

"I cut off Lily's hair—my scissors slipped, Shauna! The teacher's gonna *kill* me!"

The picture of tiny Lily bald, flashed through my head, and by that time, Mrs. Graham was at my side.

"Young man," she said to Connor. "Young man, you look at me! *RIGHT NOW!*"

Connor slid his head across my sweater slowly, until one eye was exposed.

"I'm looking," he whispered.

"Do you have any idea how much trouble you're in?" she demanded.

Connor shook his head up and down. "I think so," he whispered.

Mrs. Graham put out her big hand and clamped it around Connor's little one. "You come with me," she said and started off down the hall in the direction of the office, my little brother in tow.

I glanced back into the lunchroom where my friends watched, spellbound, through the doorway, then glanced at Mrs. Graham and my frightened brother as they went farther away from me. I decided to postpone the questions and stares from my classmates and followed my brother and Mrs. Graham to her office.

When I got to the office complex, she and Connor were already out of sight. The school secretary's seat was empty—I figured she was probably at lunch in the teacher's lounge—so there was no one to make me leave. I could hear Mrs. Graham's voice from inside the principal's office. It didn't exactly seem like eavesdropping to listen, since they were talking about my own brother. I got as close as I could to the principal's door to listen.

"And just how much did he cut off?" the principal asked. "I'm sure it was just a few hairs, right?"

"No, not right! He cut off a lot of hair, on the left side!" Mrs. Graham said. "I can't imagine how he could do that much damage with those tiny scissors in the one second my back was turned, but he did. And poor Lily was sound asleep and had no idea what was going on." Mrs. Graham's voice went up another notch. "You *have* to do something. Today! I simply *cannot* function any longer with this child in my classroom!"

Her voice kept getting higher and higher as she spoke, and I wondered if pretty soon only dogs would be able to hear it, like that special whistle my dad has at home for our dog.

Principal Forrestor stopped her before that happened. "I think the first thing to do is call in both sets of parents, Mrs. Graham, and straighten this out. Then it's probably time to set up testing for Connor. We'll make some recommendations based on what we find. You go on back to your classroom for now. Connor can stay here with me."

I ducked out of the office fast, before Mrs. Graham stormed out and caught me listening. Fortunately, sixth-grade lunch period had just ended, so I could go straight back to class without answering any questions. For now.

Wednesday was a very quiet evening at the O'Leary house. Mom and Dad came in at about 5:30 from their meeting at the school with Mr. Forrestor, Mrs. Graham, and Lily's parents. They brought Kentucky Fried Chicken for dinner, but none of us really felt like eating. Even Kevin and Tim seemed worried when I told them what Connor had done this time.

After most of the chicken was wrapped up and put away in the refrigerator, Dad put Connor to bed while I took my turn packing lunches for school the next day. Then my parents and older brothers and I had what we call a "family meeting," which either means we're planning summer vacation or somebody's in really big trouble.

"Normally, we wouldn't meet like this without the entire family present," Dad began, "but your mother and I didn't want Connor sitting here while we talk about him."

I couldn't help noticing the lines on his face while he talked. They ran like deep gullies from the sides of his nose to the corners of his mouth. I didn't remember them being there before. But to be honest, I don't usually sit around staring at him this way very often.

I glanced over at Mom and was really surprised at the way she was sitting, kind of hunched over. When we sit that way, she always rubs our backs between the shoulder blades and says in that chirpy tone of hers, "Let's sit up, now, okay? You don't want to grow up with bad posture." I opened my mouth to say it to her, but decided this might not be the best time. Meanwhile, Dad was still talking.

"You know Connor's always been an especially, um—*challenging*—child. Your mom and I hoped that this was something he might grow out of."

There was a snort from Tim's end of the table, and all our heads swung that way. Tim's face turned really red. He looked down at the table and mumbled, "Sorry. Got something in my throat."

Dad paused a minute, then went on. "Apparently, we were wrong. The school psychologist was at the meeting today, and she thinks that your little brother shows many of the symptoms of a problem called ADHD."

"Is that like a real disease? You mean he's not just a brat after all?" Tim asked. Mom and Dad both gave him that look—the one that meant you'd better change whatever it was you just said, and fast. "I mean, he's not just a—a—bad kid?"

Mom sighed the way she does when she looks in our bedrooms and can't see the floor for the mess. "No, Tim, it's not a disease. It's a disorder. ADHD stands for attention-deficit/hyperactivity disorder."

Kevin leaned forward, his elbows on the table. "Some of the kids in my class are on medication for ADHD," he said quietly. "It's the kind of thing you have for your whole life, isn't it?"

Dad nodded. "For some people, at least. We'll learn more about it later this week. Dr. Harmon's office is working on getting Connor in to see a psychiatrist on Friday."

Dr. Harmon had been our pediatrician for as long as we could remember. Knowing he was involved made the situation seem more serious somehow.

"Until then," Dad went on, "Mrs. Graham doesn't want Connor back in her class."

Tim and Kevin and I all had something to say, it seemed.

"Great. Now everybody will think we're weird!" Tim said.

"What've you got to complain about?" I asked him. "Be thankful you're in a different part of the building where people don't hear about the stuff he does."

Kevin just said, "Poor Connor. I wish we'd known sooner."

I stared at him for a moment and couldn't help thinking how grown up he was getting to be.

Thursday was not the best day of my life.

I had managed to avoid questions about Connor on Wednesday by practically running out of school the instant the bell rang. But by Thursday morning, everybody knew that Connor—*my brother*—had cut Lily's hair.

Jared kept making cracks, whenever he got near me, about how convenient it must be to have a barber in the family. Then all the sixth-grade Jared clones, who hang around him and copy everything he says, started smart-mouthing about Connor being the "baby barber" and the "wild barber of Conwell Consolidated."

Micah, who always has to go Jared one better, said, "So now, thanks to the O'Learys, the school has to install a plastic detector at the kindergarten door."

Jared looked at him, puzzled. So did all the clones.

Micah grinned. "They're supposed to screen our backpacks for dangerous weapons, aren't they? Now they'll have to get a machine that screens for *plastic scissors!*" All the girls burst out laughing, and so did most of the clones. Jared just smirked, the way he does whenever Micah upstages him.

Worst of all, though, was Leah, my supposed *friend*. There was one of those weird pauses at the lunch table—you know how everyone stops talking at the same time and the whole room goes silent? Right then, when everyone could hear her, Leah leaned across the table to me. "So when's Connor gonna do *your* hair, Shauna?" she asked in a voice that was a lot louder than it needed to be. "Just think, you might actually get a haircut that looks good for once."

Right then, I found myself wishing I didn't have a little brother—or that I had one who was normal.

Make Connections: Diagnosing ADHD

 The diagnosis of ADHD may be made by a psychiatrist, pediatrician, family doctor, or neurologist. The first task in the evaluation process will be to rule out other explanations for the child's behavior, such as emotional disorders, undetectable seizures, and poor vision or hearing. A doctor may also look at nutritional factors (for instance, too much caffeine) that might make a child overly active. Next, the professional will observe the child's behavior. She will gather information from his teachers and from family members, determining how he reacts to different situations and environments.

An accurate diagnosis is an important part of the treatment of ADHD. It allows children with this disorder to move ahead with their lives as they receive whatever combination of emotional, medical, and educational help they need.

Students with ADHD may benefit from working one-on-one with a teacher.

INDIVIDUALS WITH ADHD
HAVE LEGAL RIGHTS

Since 1973, a series of federal and state laws and court deci-
sions have supported the rights of individuals with disabilities to fully participate in all aspects of our society. Section
504 of the Rehabilitation Act of 1973, a civil rights law, pro-
hibits discrimination against individuals with disabilities, and
provides "due process" where discrimination might have oc-
curred. In 1975, the 94th Congress passed the landmark Education for the Handicapped Act, known as Public Law
94-142. Recently re-authorized as the Individuals with Disabilities Education Act (IDEA), this law provides states with
federal funds to serve the needs of individuals with disabilities, ages three to twenty-one. This service is achieved
through a very specific process defined within that law. *All
preschool and school-age students, regardless of the severity
of their disability, must be provided an "appropriate education" in the "least restrictive environment."* A multi-discipli-
nary team, which includes the parent, conducts an evaluation that identifies a student's eligibility and needs, and uses
an individualized education plan (IEP) to describe a program
that meets that student's needs. To insure that the educational program is appropriate to the child's current (and
changing) needs, programs must be reviewed at least annu-
ally, with periodic re-evaluations conducted at least every
three years.

Before these landmark laws, children with disabilities
were not guaranteed the right to an appropriate education.
Society was apt to view individuals with disabilities with sus-
picion, condemning them (or their parents) for their problems. For example, according to this way of thinking, the
child who had difficulty paying attention was not trying
hard enough, or the child who was hyperactive was "bad"
or "naughty." Fortunately, as our understanding of disorders

Research Project

We didn't have a name for ADHD until fairly recently—but that doesn't mean that people didn't have ADHD a hundred or a thousand years ago. Use the Internet to find the names of historical figures who might have had ADHD, based on descriptions of their behavior. How might their lives have been different if people had understood ADHD back then? Do you think their lives would have been better? Why or why not?

like ADHD increases, our tolerance for differences tends to expand as well.

Each state and school system has their own procedure for carrying out these laws, but basically Public Law 94-142 guarantees that the following steps will take place:

1. **Search.** Each school system will have a procedure for identifying students who might have a disability. This means that parents and teachers can refer a child they suspect may have a learning disorder to the school psychologist for diagnostic testing.
2. **Find.** Once a student with a potential problem has been identified, a system is in place for collecting information and designing an evaluation.
3. **Evaluation.** A comprehensive and multidisciplinary evaluation should be done. This will involve the school psychologist as well as teachers and other school personnel.
4. **Conference.** Parents or guardians meet with school personnel to review the evaluation conclusions, any

Text-Dependent Questions

1. What are some things that must be ruled out before a child can be diagnosed with ADHD?
2. Why is an accurate diagnosis important?
3. What is the name of the law that guarantees the educational rights of all children with disabilities.
4. How would a child with ADHD have been likely to be treated by his teacher a hundred years ago?

labels or diagnoses established, any proposed placement, and the individualized education plan (IEP). All this should be recorded in writing.

5. **Parents' decision process.** Parents or guardians decide to accept, request explanations or changes, or reject the proposed placement and IEP.
6. **Appeals process.** If parents reject the label or diagnosis, placement recommendation, or IEP, an appeals process starts with the local school and can go from there to the county or state level.
7. **Follow-up.** Progress reports are provided to the family, and a formal reevaluation is done every three years (or sooner if requested by parents or teachers). Steps 5 and 6 are then repeated before implementing the next year's plan.

Kindness is a bridge.
We are never so different from one another
that an outstretched hand can't bridge the gap.
—Joanna Mill

4

TOTALLY BLACK

When things get bad, my dad has this saying he always mis-quotes to make everybody laugh. Instead of saying, "It's always darkest just before dawn"—which Mom tells us is the way the quote *really* goes—Dad says, "It's always darkest just before it goes totally black."

It went totally black here this week.

My Great-Aunt Iris came to stay with us for the rest of last week. That's because Mrs. Graham put her foot down and said Connor absolutely was not coming back to school until my parents did something about his behavior. And because Mom and Dad have both used up their vacation and personal days at work, and they already had to take a day off to go with Connor for his meeting with the psychiatrist. So *somebody* had to stay home with Connor after he cut Lily's hair.

I offered, naturally, but it was like I'd turned invisible. Un-hear-able, too. (Is that a word, I wonder.) Mom and Dad didn't even answer me.

Anyway, Great-Aunt Iris said she'd be delighted to baby-sit; she packed up her cats and her parakeet, and moved in with us for the rest of the week.

Correction: She moved in with *me*. I'm the one with all the extra room in my bedroom, remember?

Anyway, on Friday morning, Connor met with the psychiatrist, who told my parents that, yes, Connor has ADHD. "Without a doubt," Mom and Dad quoted him to us later. When they got home, I could tell they were pretty bummed about it, but they were putting on a happy face for Connor's sake. All we heard Friday afternoon was, "Well, isn't it good that we know for sure what we're dealing with now?" and "Now we can get to work on helping you with this, Con"—that kind of stuff, all positive and upbeat.

Then my parents sat us all down and explained how, from now on, Connor would be taking a medicine called Ritalin—one that zillions of other kids in the United States and around the world are on—and that it would help him concentrate better and be a lot calmer. Tim rolled his eyes and mumbled something, but then he jerked real hard, so I knew Kevin must have kicked him under the table to shut him up.

So far, so good, right?

So why did I say it went totally black?

Because just around dinnertime, when it seemed like the O'Leary family had the Connor problem solved, the phone rang. It was Dr. Harmon, our pediatrician. My parents had asked the psychiatrist to fax his report on Connor over to the pediatrician's office, and now Dr. Harmon was very negative about putting Connor on Ritalin. My parents turned on the speakerphone so they could both talk to him at the same time, so naturally I could hear everything they said.

Turns out that Dr. Harmon has very strong opinions against using drugs like Ritalin, at least in a case like my brother's. And since he speaks with lots of italics even when he isn't upset, you can imagine how it sounded on Friday. Something like this:

"*Some*times, in very *extreme* cases, these kinds of drugs are *necessary*. But in a case like *Connor's*—where the child may be simply *high-spirited and impulsive* and *have some trouble concentrating*—it can be much, *much* better to use *behavior modification techniques*. And to *change the child's environment!*"

I wondered if that last bit meant we could send Connor to live at Great-Aunt Iris's, but no such luck. I didn't understand a lot of what I heard after that, but it sounded like Dr. Harmon wanted us to change a whole lot of things around the house—our "*environment*"—to help Connor be able to concentrate and behave better. The doctor sounded worried that, if Connor went on a medication first, lots of other ways of solving his problems could get overlooked.

The last thing I heard Dr. Harmon say before I got bored and went upstairs to vacuum up cat hair and pick parakeet feathers off my dresser, was that the least my parents should expect was that Connor would *lose his appetite* and maybe even *stop growing* if he took this medicine. Then he said he felt very, very *strongly* that my parents should try his suggestions first, before putting Connor on Ritalin.

And that was when things got really black at our house. Even though my parents didn't like the idea of their baby boy having ADHD, at least they'd thought they had the solution after seeing the psychiatrist.

Then Dr. Harmon, who they consider the best pediatrician in the entire town, maybe even the entire state, tells them their "solution" might actually hurt Connor rather than help him.

They didn't have a clue what to do next.

Things got so depressing that I spent the evening cleaning out my desk. It made me feel like at least one part of my life was in order. When I came to the drawer where I kept my old Pokemon cards, I started feeling really guilty. I pulled out ten of the very best ones—every one of them a rare—and knocked on the door of Connor's room, but there was no answer. I looked all over the house for him and finally found him out in the garage with Tim's biology project, the fifty-seven frogs he keeps in a whole bunch of aquariums. Tim and his friends have been keeping records on these frogs for weeks and weeks, like how much they eat and how much they grow—that kind of stuff. Connor likes to go and sit with the frogs sometimes, probably making up new superhero stories in his head, like "Connor, the Great Frogman, Saves the World," or something.

I held the cards out to him.

For just a second, his eyes lit up. "For me?" he said.

I shrugged. "Yeah, sure, why not? I don't need them anymore." Connor jumped up and hugged me so hard he knocked the air out of me. But when he let go, I noticed his eyes were red around the outsides.

"Have you been sitting out here crying?" I asked.

He shook his head back and forth fast, as though he wouldn't admit it even to himself, but I could see his eyes were filling up with tears.

I gave him a little one-armed hug and said, "Tell me what's the matter, bub."

It took him a minute to answer, and when he finally did, his voice sounded like someone was squeezing his throat. "I'm stupid, Shauna. I'm stupid and I'm bad, and I make everybody angry."

I was so startled I couldn't think what to say for a second. Finally, I asked him, "Why are you saying that, Connor?"

He made one of those little crying hiccups. "'Cause that's what everybody in my class says."

It was a relief to get back to school on Monday. I could get my mind off the Connor problem there, at least for a little while. It was also a relief because Great-Aunt Iris, who had returned to her own home for the weekend, was coming back that morning, parakeet, cats, and all. (*Somebody* had to stay home with Connor. Mrs. Graham's foot was still firmly down.) And guess whose room Great-Aunt Iris would be staying in again?

The excitement over Connor's lunchtime visit had died down. Lucky for me, sixth-graders don't have very long attention spans. At least, not the ones in my class. Jared's whole "baby barber" gag had pretty much died out. Now, if I could just keep him from doing anything else that would make me blip on their radar screens. I spent the better part of the day trying not to get noticed by anybody.

So you can see why I was surprised when Jock started talking to me. I guess I'd better explain who Jock is first or you won't understand how weird this is.

Jock's this kid who used to act really crazy, back when we were all in first and second grade. His name is really Jack, but Micah and Jared, nice guys that they aren't, started calling him Jock, because that's the one thing he definitely *isn't*—a jock. I remember he couldn't make a basket or field a fly ball to save his life. I also remember he used to get in trouble all the time—and I do mean *all* the time. In first grade, he spent more of the day in the time-out chair than in his own chair. In second grade, he used to brag that he and the princi-*pal* were *pals* (which he thought was the funniest joke ever) and told us that they spent so much time together they were on a first-name basis.

As I remember, Jock was supposed to get held back that year, but I don't know what happened, because when we started third grade, there he was in our class again. Somehow he just seemed to grow up and calm down over the summer. He knew the other guys in our class thought he was weird, so he hardly ever talked to them anymore. And he *never* talked to us girls—with mouths like Leah's on the loose, that would have been even more dangerous. I don't think Jock has said more than two words to me since third grade.

But there he was, talking to me at the water fountain, where we happened to be the last two people in line for a drink. Actually, since Jock had turned out to be the shortest guy in our class, he always landed at the end of the line, and that Monday, I ended up just in front of him. I had just taken this huge mouthful of water when I heard his voice behind me.

"Sorry about what happened with your little brother last week, Shauna."

I was so startled I spit all my water back in the fountain. "*What?*"

"I said I'm sorry about your brother. I kinda know how he feels." Then his ears got red and he turned and left without getting a drink.

When I walked back into the classroom, he wouldn't look at me no matter how much I stared at him. That was a trick Leah taught me back in fourth grade—if you want someone to look at you during class, just stare at him. After a while he's supposed to feel your stare and look up.

Apparently, it didn't work with Jock. Or he just didn't want to look at me. The only response I got was from the math teacher, who told me I'd been staring at Jock for half an hour and if I didn't quit, I'd have to write sentences. Everybody in class started giggling, and pretty soon Leah started passing around a note that said, "Shauna loves Jock!"

I finally cornered him by the gym door later that day. "Why did you say that about Connor before?" I demanded.

Jock looked around nervously. "'Cause I meant it. Kids like him can't help what they do, sometimes. Not if they have ADHD."

"How do *you* know he has ADHD?" I asked, angry to hear Connor's secret out in the open that way.

Jock shrugged. "Lots of us know. Because lots of us have it."

I stared at him, open-mouthed, and remembered that Jock had been the only guy in our class who didn't tease me when Connor got into trouble the week before. All of a sudden, things started making sense. "You mean *that's* why you were always in trouble in first and second grade? Because you have it, too?"

Jock nodded.

Suddenly I realized that Jock—who was one of those kids I'd just written off as not worth knowing—might have some answers that could help Connor. "But what happened? I mean, what made you stop acting so crazy?"

Jock's face got red again, and I realized how my words made him feel. Funny, I never even thought about Jock having feelings before.

That made me wonder how Connor must feel sometimes. Like when he does something crazy and we all start firing questions at him—like, "*Why* did you do that?" and "What were you *thinking?*"— but instead of answering us, he just gets all quiet. Then I started thinking about how his face looked when I ordered him not to talk to me at school. And about him saying, "I'd rather have a sister who likes me."

THE GREAT ADHD CONTROVERSY

Few medical professionals deny that ADHD exists. The existence of impulsivity and attention problems, with or without hyperactivity, is unquestionably evident in a small percentage of children.

However, some medical professionals deny that ADHD exists in the high number of cases in which it is presently being diagnosed. They feel that ADHD-like symptoms may have causes other than those cited by the medical professional majority, who are sometimes quick to diagnose ADHD and prescribe Ritalin or other stimulant drugs (which is a more than half-a-billion-dollar industry) as a treatment.

Medication offers help to children with ADHD.

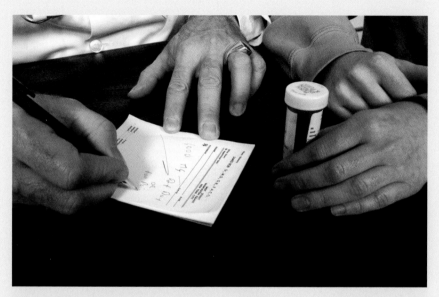

Although some people are skeptical about the role drugs should play in treating ADHD, the research indicates that these prescription drugs make a big difference in the lives of young people with this disorder.

A Nation in a Hurry?

Richard DeGrandpre, author of *Ritalin Nation,* maintains that the pace of a culture shapes its people, for good or bad, and that much of what is being diagnosed as ADHD in America today is simply a response to the incredible pace of our society.

Is ADHD a Disability?

Some people resist thinking of ADHD as a disability. For example, CH.A.D.D. (Children and Adults with Attention Deficit/Hyperactivity Disorder) stresses that all people with ADHD have many talents and abilities that they can use to enhance their lives. In fact, CH.A.D.D. says,

many people with ADHD even feel that their patterns of behavior give them unique, often unrecognized, advantages.
People with ADHD tend to be outgoing and ready for action. Because of their drive for excitement and stimulation,
many become successful in business, sports, construction,
and public speaking. Because of their ability to think about
many things at once, many have won acclaim as artists and
inventors.

Most researchers, however, and many professionals who
work in the field of special education believe that ADHD is
indeed a disability that needs to be treated. In 1998, the National Institutes of Health held a conference on ADHD. It
was attended by more than one thousand experts in the
fields of pediatrics to psychiatry. The consensus statement
that grew out of this conference holds that ADHD is a true
disorder—and that medications and therapy can be used
effectively to treat it.

MEDICATE—OR NOT?

Another ADHD controversy has arisen over whether to treat
it with drugs. Many parents and some physicians favor finding alternatives to drug therapy for children with ADHD.
  However, most scientific researchers today agree that
medication is the best treatment option for children and
adolescents with ADHD. Many children with ADHD who
have not been treated will eventually have higher rates of:

- substance abuse
- academic and professional failure
- relationship problems
- legal problems

Research indicates that treating ADHD with stimulants actually decreases the risk of alcohol- and substance-use disorders—while adolescents with ADHD who are left untreated have much higher rates of:

- car accidents
- school failure
- speeding tickets

A large study that compared treatment methods for ADHD found that medication alone and medication plus intensive behavioral therapy proved to be equal in effectiveness—and both were superior to behavioral treatment alone and community-based treatment.

Other studies indicate the toll taken on families where a child with ADHD is left untreated:

- parents often have to reduce their work hours
- parents may be forced to change jobs or stop working altogether
- parents experience high levels of marital discord

According to many medical experts, physicians who recommend alternative treatments are doing their patients a disservice. Mary Ann Johnson, a professional in the field, summarizes this viewpoint:

These physicians have no scientific data to back up their opinions. While they are entitled to their opinions, the media coverage of this "anti-ADHD diagnosis and treatment" often leaves those that are not educated on the subject with misinformation and fear of treatment.

Myths About Psychostimulant Medications

Myth: Can lead to drug addiction later in life.
Fact: Since these drugs help many children succeed better at school, home, and play, avoiding negative experiences may actually help prevent future addictions to harmful drugs.

Myth: Responding well to this medication means a person has ADHD.
Fact: These medications allow many people to focus better, whether or not they have ADHD, but the improvement is more noticeable in people with ADHD.

Medication can help children with ADHD be able to sit quietly at a desk during school hours.

Myth: Medication should be stopped when a child reaches adolescence.
Fact: About 80 percent of those who needed medication as children still need it as teenagers, and 50 percent will need it as adults.

Myth: Medication will make children "foggy" and dull-acting.
Fact: Children with ADHD who take these medications usually seem more alert, since they are better able to focus and pay attention.

Myth: These drugs have dangerous side effects.
Fact: Research indicates that these drugs are safe. They are quickly excreted by the body, and the side effects they may have are usually mild and do not threaten a child's well-being, provided they are taken as directed.
(Adapted from the National Institute of Mental Health's "Attention Deficit Hyperactivity Disorder." NIH Publication No. 96-3572.)

How Many Children with ADHD Take Medication?

When parents were also asked about whether their child was taking medication for ADHD, here were the results:

- The prevalence of children 4 to 17 years of age taking ADHD medication increased from 4.8 percent in 2007 to 6.1 percent in 2011.

- More US children were receiving ADHD treatment in 2011 compared to 2007; however, as many as 17.5 percent of children with current ADHD were not

Text-Dependent Questions

1. What does author Richard DeGrandpre believe is causing ADHD?
2. Why do some people not believe that ADHD is a disability? What do they believe instead?
3. List at least five reasons why ADHD medication appears to be appropriate for most kids with ADHD.
4. If you were a child with ADHD, would you be more liked to be taking medication if you lived in Louisiana or Nevada?

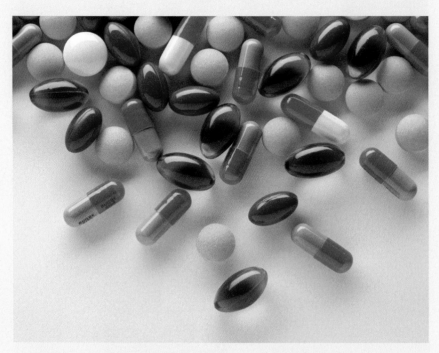

Medication is not a magic answer to ADHD, but it does offer a practical answer to many of ADHD's symptoms.

Research Project

ADHD medications are helpful to children who have ADHD. But they're not helpful for young adults who take these drugs recreationally. Go online or use the library to find out more about the abuse of Ritalin and other ADHD medications. Report what you find to your class.

receiving either medication for ADHD or mental health counseling in 2011.

- In 2011, the percentage of children taking medication for ADHD was not the same across the United States. It ranged from a low of 2 percent in Nevada to a high of 10.4 percent in Louisiana.

Words to Understand

stimulant: Something that produces a temporary increase in activity.

neurotransmitter: A biochemical substance that transmits or inhibits nerve impulses at a synapse.

brain stem: The part of the brain that connects the spinal cord to the brain.

cortex: The outer layer of the brain.

norepinephrine: One of the neurotransmitters.

serotonin: A chemical that influences the sleep-wake cycle, depression, and obsessive-compulsive disorder, among other things.

antidepressants: Medications used to treat depression.

antihypertensives: Medications used to treat high blood pressure.

antipsychotics: Medications used to treat psychoses (for example, schizophrenia).

noradrenergic reuptake inhibitor: A substance that slows the reabsorption of norepinephrine.

tics: Involuntary body movements.

neurons: The nerve cell body and all its processes.

synapse: The tiny space between one nerve cell and other cells (nerve, muscle, etc.) through which nerve impulses are transmitted.

antisocial: Against the basic principles of society.

5

FINDING ANSWERS

As bad as it made me feel to embarrass Jock, I still had to find out what he knew about ADHD in case it could help Connor. I tried my question again, only this time I left out the word "crazy."

"Jock, remember how you used to get sent to the principal's office all the time?" I asked, hoping that sounded better.

Jock rolled his eyes. "You think I could forget?"

"So what happened to you? I mean, you hardly ever get in trouble anymore. How'd you stop doing all that dumb—I mean, that— stuff?" Funny how, half an hour ago, I couldn't have cared less about Jock's feelings. Actually, I'd never even thought about him *having* any feelings, to tell you the truth, but now it seemed important to be really careful about what I said.

I guess I just didn't want to see the same hurt on his face I'd seen on Connor's. The hurt *I'd* caused.

"My parents took me to a clinic in New York, and when they decided I had ADHD, they put me on some medicine. Don't you remember how I had to always stop at the nurse's office on the way to lunch?"

I shook my head back and forth.

"I wasn't the only one, either," Jock went on. "There were two other kids from our class who had to go with me so we could get our medicine every day."

A light went on in my head. "You mean Kelly, right? And Micah, too."

Jock nodded.

"None of us ever knew why you guys were getting medicine," I said. "You never answered us when we asked what you were doing."

"Why should I?" Jock countered. "It would have only meant more teasing, and I got enough of that!"

"And Micah and Kelly never really said much when we asked them, just that they had to take medicine to help them listen better. After a while, we just got used to you being a couple of minutes late for lunch and forgot about it."

"That's because the teachers tried to help by not making a big deal of it, and—"

"Wait a minute," I broke in. "Micah and Kelly couldn't have the same thing *you* do. I mean, they never acted craz—" I bit my lip.

This time, though, Jock just grinned. "They never acted 'crazy,' like me, so they couldn't have ADHD, is that what you mean?"

Now it was my turn to be embarrassed.

"There's more than one kind of ADHD. Having it doesn't mean you're always bouncing off the walls and doing stupid things. Some people have the kind where you can't concentrate very well. Like, you keep daydreaming, or thinking about other things even when you don't want to. And sometimes, when people tell you things you maybe don't remember what they said very well."

"My brother does all those things, " I said, "*plus* acting hyper!"

"Some people have some of the symptoms, and others—" He stopped and then he grinned at me again. "Well, I guess some people just have it all, like me."

I stared at him for a minute, and then we both burst out laughing. I could hardly believe my ears. I mean, who would've dreamed that Jock could be funny?

"Okay, if that's all true, how come you and Micah and Kelly don't go to the nurse's office at lunch anymore?"

"The medicine they used to give us didn't last very long, so we had to take it every four hours or so. But now they have different kinds of medicine, and some of them last all day. They even make things called transdermal patches." He pointed to his ribs on his left side. "You can stick them on and leave them for a whole day."

"What's a patch got to do with ADHD?" I asked.

"There's medicine in it, and it kind of soaks in through your skin, a little bit at a time," Jock explained. "When the medicine's all used up, you put another patch on.

"You don't have to swallow any pills?" I asked.

"Nope."

That afternoon, it felt like I had some sort of strange glasses on when I looked around at the other sixth-graders, because they all looked kind of different to me. I guess there were a couple of reasons for that, and I tried to write them down in my diary at home before I forgot them.

The first reason I wrote down was finding out that Jock—who everybody laughs at behind his back and hardly anyone will even talk to—was really not so bad. After all, he was the only one who hadn't teased me about Connor, like I said before. And he'd been through a lot of teasing himself and managed to keep going. He could even be funny. So why haven't any of us ever taken the time to find that out, I wondered?

The second reason I wrote down was this: I was starting to get the idea that lots of other people had problems, too. All this time, I'd been worrying that if people found out about Connor, they wouldn't want to be around *me* anymore. But other people, like Kelly and Micah, had problems, too. But they still had friends. And Jock probably would, too, if he ever starting talking to us again.

Then I started thinking that maybe having Connor for a brother wasn't so bad. I wrote down, "Connor isn't so bad, really. He *could* be the kind of kid who burns down buildings, or hurts cats, or something. *That* would be a big problem. Compared to that, Connor just has little problems."

Then I remembered about Connor cutting Lily's hair. "Okay," I wrote, "make that *medium*-sized problems."

It was a little less gloomy at home that evening. The fact that Great-Aunt Iris, her cats, and her parakeet were back—in my room—didn't bother me as much this time. She really loved Connor, and he seemed a lot happier when she was around. I think it was because of how she always took the time to listen to everything he said, and she never rolled her eyes (at least I never saw her) when he told her his latest crazy idea. Sometimes, she even imagined right along with him, and they made up stories together. Then she'd tell him he had the best imagination she'd ever heard, and she'd sit down at the computer and let him dictate his story to her, typing away as fast as she could (which wasn't very fast, since she only used her two index fingers).

After dinner, I was loading the dishwasher while Mom and Dad and Great-Aunt Iris sat around the kitchen table, drinking coffee and tea and discussing what to do about Connor.

Dad was all for starting Ritalin, like the psychiatrist prescribed. Mom was all for "changing our home environment," the way Dr. Harmon wanted. Great-Aunt Iris sipped tea quietly until I finished loading all the dishes and was starting to wipe down the counters and the stovetop. By then, the discussion was heating up considerably, with Mom and Dad both arguing their side of the question over and over again.

I finally heard Great-Aunt Iris's voice break in, and I stopped wiping, mid-counter, at the tone of her voice. Mom and Dad both turned to look at her, too, their faces tight and exasperated-looking. "You're just arguing in circles, and that'll get you nowhere," she said. "You might try striking a compromise."

"What kind of compromise?" Mom asked.

"Why not try your pediatrician's ideas first if you're so worried about using the medicine? Go ahead and change a few things around here. If that helps Connor, great. If it doesn't, then you go ahead with the medicine."

They talked for another hour or so—it always amazes me how long parents can spend talking over one little thing—but they finally took her advice. They set up another meeting, this time with all the school people involved and the psychiatrist and the pediatrician.

I just wish I'd known ahead of time how much that meeting was going to change our "home environment!"

MEDICATIONS

The drug most often used to treat ADHD is methylphenidate hydrochloride, which was introduced under the name Ritalin® in the early 1960s. It quickly became the preferred drug for calming hyperactivity, replacing other drugs such as benzedrine.

Methylphenidate hydrochloride is a central nervous system **stimulant** and blocks the reuptake of dopamine, a **neurotransmitter**, into presynaptic neurons. Researchers are not yet certain how methylphenidate works to increase attention, but it has been assumed for some time that the drug stimulates the **brain stem** and the **cortex**. Recent studies appear to support this theory. It may seem odd that medications known for their stimulating effects can also calm people. Researchers think that, in people with ADHD, stimulants such as methylphenidate improve concentration, which in turn tones down the impulsivity and distractibility of the disorder.

Another stimulant used frequently to treat ADHD is Adderall®, a combination of amphetamine and dextroamphetamine. Dextroamphetamine is sometimes used alone and sometimes in combination with amphetamine, as in Adderall. According to Edward Drummond, M.D., in *The Complete Guide to Psychiatric Drugs,* these two drugs are mirror images of each other, and there is evidence that some patients benefit from the combination. Adderall works by releasing dopamine and **norepinephrine** from presynaptic neurons. When used at high doses, it also causes the release of **serotonin**. Several clinical studies have established Adderall as a safe and efficient drug for this disorder.

Other classes of medications sometimes used in the treatment of ADHD include **antidepressants**, **antihypertensives**, and **antipsychotics**.

In cases where stimulants don't work or they cause unpleasant side effects, nonstimulant drugs might help. The first nonstimulant medication approved by the FDA was Strattera®. It's now used in children, adolescents, and adults. The FDA then approved a second nonstimulant drug, Intuniv®, for children and teens between ages six and seventeen, followed by the non-stimulant Kapvay for use alone or in combination with a stimulant to increase its effectiveness. These medications can all improve concentration and impulse control in children with ADHD.

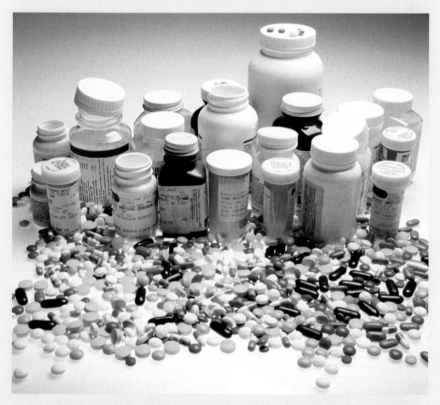

A variety of medications are being studied for treating ADHD.

Make Connections:
Side Effects of Stimulant Drugs

Stimulants have a minimum of side effects. These drugs can:

- cause mild loss of appetite
- worsen existing tics or cause new ones
- retard growth
- worsen or cause psychotic thinking and manic episodes
- cause seizures (but the risk is minimal)

Any medication is capable of producing side effects. Many have risk factors. The best way for individuals to protect their health is to educate themselves about all possible side effects and to communicate regularly with their doctor.

INSIDE THE BRAIN

To understand how any psychiatric drug works, it helps to have a basic idea of what goes on inside the brain. The central nervous system, which includes both the brain and the spinal cord, is the communications center of the human body. Messages, known as neural impulses, travel through the body to the spine and brain via the *neurons*, specialized cells that function as links in this vast communication network. For instance, when a person's finger touches a hot stove, messages that the finger is in pain fly from the finger, up the arm, and to the central nervous system via the spinal cord. Signals are then sent from the central nervous system back to the arm and finger, telling them to move—very quickly—out of harm's way. Because each neuron is in

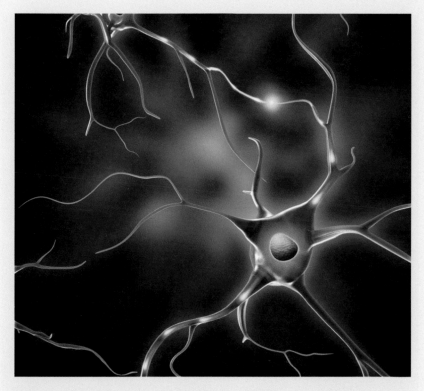

Nerve cells pass messages between them, but between each cell is a tiny gap. Neurotransmitters carry the messages across this gap.

contact with many other neurons, there are multi-millions of such interconnections throughout the body.

Neurons communicate messages by sending electrical signals from neuron to neuron. In between these special cells is a tiny space called a **synapse**, and it is through this space that nerve impulses travel, jumping from cell to cell in much the same way an electric current jumps from point to point. When a message is sent, a neuron is said to "fire," re- leasing chemical substances called neurotransmitters that

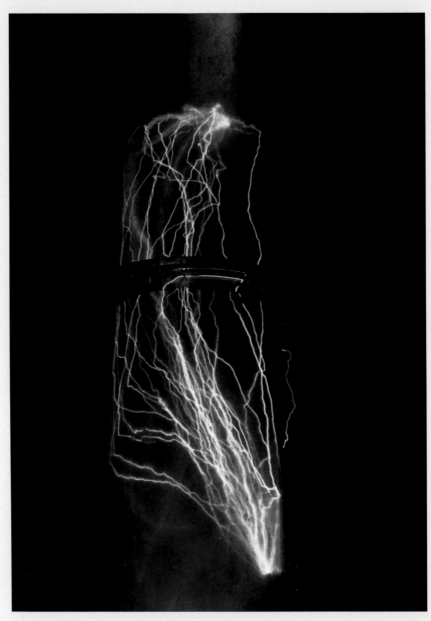

The messages sent by our nerves are like tiny bursts of electricity.

make jumping the synapse possible. These chemical substances then cross from the presynaptic neuron (the sending brain cell) to the postsynaptic neuron (the receiving brain cell), where they bind themselves to the appropriate chemical receptor and influence the behavior of this second neuron by either helping the message along or by inhibiting the passage of the message. There are many neurotransmitters, and each one produces different effects. Psychiatric drugs sometimes increase the proportion of specific neurotransmitters by blocking the neuron's ability to absorb or reabsorb these substances, thus temporarily affecting the ability of the brain to transmit neural impulses.

WORDS THAT SHAPE REALITY

Rethinking Terms

A different and more positive way to think about children with learning and behavioral differences, that recognizes the strengths they so frequently have, is suggested by educator Mary Sheedy Kurcinka in the book *Raising Your Spirited Child*. She recommends replacing the following negative terms with the positive terms to their right:

Instead of saying, The child . . .	try saying, The child. . .
is wild	is energetic
is demanding	has high standards
is stubborn	is tenacious
is anxious	is cautious
is picky	is selective
is explosive	is dramatic
is loud	is enthusiastic, full of zest
is aggressive	is assertive

Research Project

Read about another boy who is a little like Connor. See if your library has this book:

Joey Pigza Swallowed the Key by Jack Gantos

If you can't find it, ask your librarian if she can order it for you or recommend a similar book. Here's the publisher's description of the book:

Joey Pigza can't sit still. He can't pay attention, he can't follow the rules, and he can't help it—especially when his meds aren't working. Joey's had problems ever since he was born, problems just like his dad and grandma have. And whether he's wreaking havoc on a class trip or swallowing his house key, Joey's problems are getting worse. Joey knows he's really a good kid, but no matter how hard he tries to do the right thing, something always seems to go wrong. Will he ever get anything right?

Positive Words

According to Thomas Armstrong, Ph.D, in *The Myth of the A.D.D. Child*, a study conducted by Jan Loney at the University of Iowa showed that fifth- and sixth-graders classed as hyperactive "scored significantly lower on a self-esteem inventory than so-called normal students at the same age." The fact that younger children, also considered hyperactive, did not show the same lower levels of self-esteem, led to the conclusion that "children develop lower self-esteem as a

Make Connections: In the Classroom

Young children with ADHD benefit from:
- a highly structured environment
- specific, brief directions
- interventions to reduce classroom disruptions

result of the kinds of negative experiences they accumulate from home and school as they grow up."

Positive words—those that grow out of true appreciation for who another person is—can make a great difference in a child's self-esteem. Statements that validate another person can help build his or her sense of being someone with worth.

SOCIAL RELATIONSHIPS AND ADHD

Aggressive behavior is often characteristic of children with ADHD, along with inattentiveness and hyperactivity. Because children with ADHD are often "thrill seekers" (according to Kenneth W. Merrell, in the *Journal of Emotional and Behavioral Disorders*, winter 2001), they may operate on a different social agenda than do other children. They may actually enjoy domineering others and may find that impulsive behavior is motivational in nature, thus leading researchers to conclude, "it is not that children with ADHD cannot delay responses, it is that they don't want to."

ADHD and aggression are closely associated, a fact that indicates an increased risk of developing ***antisocial***

Kids with ADHD may be more likely to get in fights. This has to do with their inability to control their impulses.

Text-Dependent Questions

1. Which drug is used most often to treat ADHD? What are other ADHD medications?
2. Explain the word "side effects" in relation to ADHD medication.
3. Why are neurotransmitters so important?
4. Describe some ways that language can shape the reality of a child with ADHD.

problems in those with ADHD. These problems do not diminish over time, but commonly continue into adolescence and the adult years.

Merrell writes that "one result of poor social skills, including aggression, inattentiveness, and hyperactivity, is that these characteristics lead to rejection by peers." Rejection by peers at an early age can lead to negative circumstances later in life; children with ADHD who often face such rejection may have fewer friends and may experience low self-esteem.

Any real change implies the breakup of the world as one has known it.
—James Baldwin

6

CHANGES

The way I see it, Connor's the one with the problem so Connor's the one who should have to change, right? Wrong.

At least, according to my parents it's wrong. They have this idea that Connor's ADHD might be the result of things in our family, like the way we live and stuff. So according to them, our whole family needs to change, not just Connor.

They had a big meeting with Dr. Harmon and the psychiatrist and the school people, and agreed to try a compromise, like Great-Aunt Iris suggested, to see if they could work out Connor's problems without using drugs. If that doesn't work, then they'll try Ritalin, too.

Dr. Harmon gave my parents a "lifestyle checklist" to fill out, and a bunch of books about ADHD and how to treat it without drugs. After we read the books, we're supposed to work through the checklist, which asks way too many personal questions, if you want my opinion (which nobody does these days, I might add). We're supposed to go over our filled-out checklist with Dr. Harmon, and then we'll decide what changes we should make to help Connor.

The first big change around our house was that TV, as we knew it, was over.

We have three TVs downstairs—one in the kitchen, one in the living room, and one in the family room—and at least two are on nearly all the time. That seems about right to me, but Dr. Harmon has different ideas about these things, and he talked my parents into putting away two of the TVs and hardly ever turning the other one on. He calls it the "TV diet." Funny. Very funny.

Changing the TV situation downstairs was bad enough, let me tell you, but when it came to the TVs *upstairs*, Dr. Harmon's ideas got *really* different. In fact, they got downright annoying. In our family the rule has always been that when you turn thirteen, you get your own TV for your bedroom. So, guess who's turning thirteen this summer? And guess who's been looking forward to having her own TV in her bedroom for *twelve whole years*? And now, just because of the Connor problem, I probably won't get it. You can guess how I feel about this, can't you? I thought so.

When they told me, I threatened to go on strike, so Dad put the pressure on. "Kevin and Tim have already agreed to take the TVs out of their rooms, Shauna," he said. Then he looked at me, as though waiting for me to sign on to the program.

"That makes absolutely no sense!" I started out yelling, but remembered in time how freaked both Dad and Mom get if we yell. It's not "respectful," they always tell us. So I lowered my voice, then went on. "How is it going to help Connor if Kevin and Tim and I give up TVs in our bedrooms?"

Dad rubbed his chin the way he always does when he's thinking. "It probably won't help him directly."

I folded my arms across my chest and grinned. Victory was in sight!

"However," Dad went on, "what we're trying to do is change the whole atmosphere of our home. And we can't do that unless everyone cooperates. See, Shauna, some people think TV and videos are actually changing the way modern human beings think. Because of the rapid way messages come through on TV and videos, our brains have adapted to processing information at a higher speed. And so much information, at such a rapid-fire pace, is creating a whole generation of kids who need constant overstimulation to keep concentrating."

My eyes were glazing over. I wanted more than anything to escape this lecture, but I knew it was a really bad time to zone out in front of Dad. I didn't understand most of what he said, but it was all about how having a shorter attention span could produce some of the same symptoms as ADHD, like having trouble paying attention in class, for instance.

About fifteen minutes later, I could tell by his tone that he was starting the wrap-up. "So you see, Shauna, we can't really expect Connor to accept a lifestyle with less media stimulation if we don't ask you and your older brothers to do the same thing."

Now I'll translate for you: these days, about the only time the TV goes on is when my parents decide there's something worthwhile that we should all watch together. This past weekend, for instance, Dad brought home a video of *Babe*, that movie about the pig that herds sheep, and we watched it. (Of course, Kevin and Tim and I still watch TV as much as ever at our friends' houses, but we don't feel the need to point that out to Mom and Dad right now, what with the stress they're under and all.)

They've even started reading books to us in the evening. At first I thought it was really dumb, sitting around in the family room being read to like a little kid again. But when Dad started reading *The Hobbit,* I have to admit I kind of got hooked. So did Tim and Kevin, and of course, Connor loves it—mostly because he gets to help build a fire in the fireplace first, and then he throws popcorn to the dog most of the time Dad's reading. But he does listen.

Now that you know what's happened with the TV, I'm sure you can guess what happened to Nintendo. It's not as bad for me as it is for Tim and Kevin, because I never cared much about Nintendo, but it's a big change for the guys, I can tell you. Now they only play on the weekend and only after all the homework is done. And when they do play, Dad has started playing with them. He says he wants to know more about what's going on in his kids' lives.

The third big change at our house is that nobody teases Connor anymore—at ALL. We're not supposed to give him any stress. There are a *lot* of questions on Dr. Harmon's checklist about family stress. These are the kinds of things we had to answer:

Are you going through a divorce? (I checked with Mom and Dad separately, just to make sure there were no surprises in the works.)

Are you experiencing conflict in your family? (I said we should write, "Only when my three brothers are around," but nobody laughed.)

Is your family having financial problems? (See what I mean about personal questions?)

Has a family member recently died?

Etc., etc.

When I asked Mom why they wanted to know all this stuff, she said that one of the theories about ADHD is that a very big percentage of kids who have the signs of ADHD—restlessness, difficulty concentrating, and irritating behavior—sometimes act that way because they're either "depressed or extremely anxious" over problems at home. So I figure it ought to be Kevin and Tim and me who show the symptoms of ADHD, actually, but I guess that's not the way it works.

Not only are we not supposed to tease Connor anymore, we're each supposed to say four or five positive things to him every week. Like, how we think he's a really creative kid. Or how he did the best job setting the table that we've ever seen. Or, "Oh, good, you remembered to feed the dog without anybody reminding you today." That kind of stuff. Mom says it's important because sometimes, kids with ADHD spend so much time in trouble that they get a really low opinion of themselves, and the worse you feel about yourself, the more likely you are to just quit trying.

After about two months of all these changes, Connor started going to a martial arts class. It's supposed to help him "channel" his energy better, and Tim and Kevin and Dad and I go with him because Mom and Dad think he'll do better if we're all involved. They also have this new thing where they send Connor to run around the house when he gets too hyper. The running seems to soak up some of his extra energy, like a piece of bread in gravy, and when he comes back in, he controls himself better.

Speaking of gravy, did I mention the big change in our diet? Not the kind of diet where you get a skinny body, but the kind where you only eat stuff that's good for you—especially at breakfast. And it turns out that what is good for you, if you're a kid with ADHD, can be a lot less carbs and sugary stuff (which means I got to kiss my favorite breakfast cereal and Mom's homemade cinnamon rolls goodbye, except on weekends), and a whole lot more protein and fruit and complex carbs, which are supposed to help you pay attention better. So now we have—get this—bean burritos for breakfast some days. And eggs and ham, too, stuff like that. But burritos? Oh come on!

Anyway, there've been a lot of other changes at our house, and my parents are all excited about helping Connor conquer his problem. He's been doing really well at home, especially with Great-Aunt Iris here to pay extra attention to him.

But school is another story.

ADHD PLUS SOMETHING ELSE

Some children with ADHD also have other illnesses or conditions. For example, they may have one or more of the following:

- A learning disability. A child in preschool with a learning disability may have difficulty understanding certain sounds or words or have problems expressing himself or herself in words. A school-aged child may struggle with reading, spelling, writing, and math.

- Oppositional defiant disorder. Kids with this condition, in which a child is overly stubborn or rebellious, often argue with adults and refuse to obey rules.

- Conduct disorder. This condition includes behaviors in which the child may lie, steal, fight, or bully others. He or she may destroy property, break into homes, or carry or use weapons. These children or teens are also

at a higher risk of using illegal substances. Kids with conduct disorder are at risk of getting into trouble at school or with the police.

- Anxiety and depression. Treating ADHD may help to decrease anxiety or some forms of depression.

- Bipolar disorder. Some children with ADHD may also have this condition in which extreme mood swings go from mania (an extremely high elevated mood) to depression in short periods of time.

- Tourette syndrome. Very few children have this brain disorder, but among those who do, many also have ADHD. Some people with Tourette syndrome have nervous tics and repetitive mannerisms, such as eye blinks, facial twitches, or grimacing. Others clear their throats, snort, or sniff frequently, or bark out words inappropriately. These behaviors can be controlled with medication.

(Adapted from the National Institute of Mental Health's Attention Deficit Hyperactivity Disorder website.)

What we see depends mainly on what we look for.
—John Lubbock

7

ACCEPTANCE

At first, we were all really hopeful that all the changes we'd made at home were going to change the way Connor acted at school. From what I could see of him in the lunchroom and on the playground, he seemed a little calmer. A *little*. If you don't count the paper airplane he made out of his "Color the Zoo Animals" handout—the airplane that hit Mrs. Graham in the forehead. Also, you probably shouldn't count the flying carrot stick incident in the lunchroom. The way I see it, Connor was just doing research on flight.

Then came Monday, the day Tim and his best friends, Jason and Danny, were supposed to present their project in biology class. They had taken their frogs—all fifty-seven of them—into school early Monday morning and set up the aquariums in the biology room. Down at the end of our hall, fifty-five of the frogs were now croaking happily. (Two died from the shock of being moved, according to Tim, so I guess you could say they croaked *unhappily*—get it? They really *croaked*.)

Unfortunately, Monday was also the day that Mrs. Graham decided to try Mom's suggestion about letting Connor run off some energy if he got too hyper in class. The problem was, it was raining, so she couldn't really send him outside. Instead, she told him to go to the gym and run five laps. It was just about lunchtime, and she knew the gym would be empty.

Knowing Mrs. Graham, I'm sure she said something like, "Walk very quietly to the gym, Connor. Do not run in the halls! Save your running for when you get—to—the—gym."

So he did, or at least that's how he explained it to us later. "I walked so quiet that I heard the frogs croaking when I passed the biology room. So I wanted to say hello to them 'cuz I knew they were lonesome 'cuz there wasn't anybody in the room with them. And when I saw them, they looked really sad, so I thought I'd just let them out for a little recess."

Once Connor saw the frogs, the rest was inevitable, I guess. (That's a vocabulary word we had last week. It means that after what he did next, there was no escaping what followed—and it was all over for me in the sixth grade.)

"Letting them out just took a minute," Connor added (as though that would help us understand somehow), and the more he told us, the faster his words came out, until they all ran together, "and then I was gonna go right to the gym. Really. So I wasn't disobeying Mrs. Graham or anything. I just opened the screens on the top of the 'quariams, and then I could get the frogs out real easy. But then theywouldn'tgooutsidelikeItoldthemto!"

When Connor engineered the great frog escape, three things happened at once:

Number one, frogs started hopping down the hall in fifty-five directions.

Number two, Connor started running around in circles, trying to "herd them together like Babe!" he told us later.

And number three, the sixth grade got dismissed to go to lunch. So my whole class walked out the door of our room and right into a frog stampede.

Dad says you can learn something from every experience. I learned you can't herd frogs.

Emancipated frogs jump around like popcorn in hot oil. It took about three seconds for every sixth-grade guy to decide to "help" Connor by running down the hall full speed and lunging at all fifty-five frogs.

It took another half a second for every sixth-grade girl to start screaming at the top of her lungs. Every girl except me. I just cried because I could see my last chance to ever be a normal sixth-grader fading away. (Or should I make that, *hopping* away?)

Mom and Dad arrived at school faster than you would have thought possible. I tagged along to the principal's office to hear what came next, and things were so confused that nobody noticed me for a minute. They barely got inside the door of the main office before everyone started talking at once.

What Mrs. Graham had to say was pretty dramatic—lots of italics, you know? I think she might be taking lessons from Dr. Harmon. At any rate, she kept saying that Connor *needs* to be on medicine. The principal was a lot calmer, and so was the school psychologist—who was also there—but they both seemed to agree: Connor really needed to take medicine to help him control his impulses.

I could see Mom and Dad were sad. They had tried so hard to help Connor without medicine, and it seemed like it was working—at least partly. Even I could tell he was behaving better, and he could pay attention to things longer. But he still didn't stop and figure out when his behavior made sense and when it didn't.

Finally, the principal took charge and started motioning everyone involved to chairs in his office. That's when they noticed me.

"Shauna!" Dad said, "What are *you* doing here?"

I wasn't very pleased when they sent me back to class, for two reasons. Number one, I really wanted to see what they were going to do to Connor this time. Number two, facing the other sixth-graders wasn't very high on my list of things to do just then.

My class was working on country projects when I got back. Everybody had to choose a country in the Western Hemisphere and do a poster on it. I kept my head down and got right to work drawing in little upside-down Vs to represent the mountain ranges in Colombia.

Everything was good until another teacher came to the door and Mrs. Rose stepped out in the hall to talk to her. The minute she was outside the door, Jared turned to me. "So how's it feel, Shauna? Having Dr. Doolittle for a brother, I mean?" In case you don't remember, Dr. Doolittle's the guy in the movie who talks to the animals and they all follow him around.

Everybody burst out laughing, except for Jock. He sits three rows away, and when I glanced at him, he winked at me like he knew how I was feeling.

Then Kelly chimed in. "Yeah, Shauna, why didn't you tell us you had such a famous brother?"

"And multitalented, too," said Micah. "A couple months ago he was gonna be a barber, remember?"

I kept adding mountains to Colombia, but now I was pressing so hard they were making dents in the posterboard. I looked at Jock again, and he shook his head back and forth, telling me not to let them get to me.

But when Leah—that would be my *best friend*, Leah—swiveled around in her desk and asked, "So how does it feel to have such a weirdo for a brother, Shauna?" I'd had enough.

I put down my marker, slowly and deliberately. Then I stood up and faced the whole class. "My brother, Connor, has ADHD. That stands for attention-deficit/hyperactivity disorder. He's smart, he's funny, he's very creative, and he's not weird. He has trouble sitting still sometimes and paying attention. And sometimes he does things before he thinks.

"But I'll tell you one thing Connor *isn't*—he isn't mean! And he doesn't call people names. And he doesn't even know how to make fun of them. So you tell me why you call *him* weird. I'd say all of you have a bigger problem when it comes to weirdness!"

For just a minute, everybody in the class was absolutely still. My life was over anyway, so I figured I might as well keep going.

"And another thing—some of you in this classroom have the same problem Connor does, but you keep it a big secret because you know that if other people find out, you'll get teased and talked about the same way you're talking about my brother." I could see Jock giving me a double thumbs-up. "And when you find out somebody *does* have ADHD, you treat him so bad he doesn't even feel like he can talk in class anymore. Well, I think we *need* to talk about it, right out in the open."

I heard the door close softly and saw Mrs. Rose standing just inside. She walked to the front of the room and smiled at me. "Thank you, Shauna. Class, I think this might be a good time to put away our country projects and have a class meeting."

You know, if you'd told me, that morning when I woke up, that I would say those kinds of things to my entire class before the day was over, I would have said you were crazy. This was definitely not in my game plan for looking like a normal sixth-grader. But all of a sudden, when I saw Connor in the hall with fifty-five frogs hopping every which way, I realized that looking like a normal sixth-grader didn't really matter to me anymore—at least, not as much as being a good big sister.

THE SCHOOL EXPERIENCE

The most important non-medication treatment for children with ADHD usually occurs in the classroom. Although parents have the option of taking their child to a private practitioner for evaluation and educational services, most children with ADHD qualify for free services within the public schools. There, steps will be taken to ensure that each child with ADHD receives an education that meets his or her unique needs. For example, the special education teacher, working with parents, the school psychologist, school administrators, and the classroom teacher must assess the child's strengths and weaknesses and design an Individualized Educational Program (IEP). The IEP outlines the specific skills the child needs to develop as well as appropriate learning activities that build on the child's strengths. Parents play an important role in the process. They must be included in

meetings and given an opportunity to review and approve their child's IEP.

Individualized Education Plan (IEP)

An IEP should include these points:

1. A statement of the child's current level of education performance.
2. A statement of yearly goals or achievements expected for each area of identified weakness by the end of the school year.
3. Short-term objectives stated in instructional terms (concrete, observable steps leading to the mastery of the yearly goals).
4. A statement of the specific special education and support services to be provided to the child.
5. A statement of the extent to which a child will be able to participate in regular education programs and justification for any special placement recommended.
6. Projected dates for the beginning of services and how long they are anticipated to last.
7. A statement of the criteria and evaluation procedures to be used in determining (on at least an annual basis, if not more frequently) whether the short-term objectives have been achieved.

Legal Protection

Many children with ADHD or other disabilities are able to receive such special education services under the Individuals with Disabilities Education Act (IDEA) (discussed in chapter 3). Children who do not qualify for services under IDEA can receive help under an earlier law, the National Rehabilitation Act, Section 504, which defines disabilities more broadly.

Qualifying for services under the National Rehabilitation Act is often called "504 eligibility."

Because ADHD is a disability that affects children's ability to learn and interact with others, it can certainly be a disabling condition. Under one law or another, most children can receive the services they need.

OTHER TREATMENTS FOR ADHD

Other kinds of treatments may also be helpful for children with ADHD. Psychotherapy, or counseling, helps children with ADHD to feel good about themselves and accept their disorder. Behavior modification techniques may help these children change their actual behaviors by giving praise or rewards every time they act in a desired way. Social skills training may also help these children learn new behaviors by practicing skills like sharing, taking turns, and learning to read others' facial expressions and tone of voice. Support groups can also help children with ADHD and their parents to feel better about their problems and understand that they are not alone. Parenting-skills training gives parents tools for managing their children's behavior, like "time out," behavior modification techniques, and stress management techniques to help both their children and themselves handle their frustrations more effectively.

Because children with ADHD cannot self-regulate their emotions or behavior easily, the best support these children can be given involves structuring their environments, both at home and at school. Children with ADHD need reliable, consistent reinforcement for appropriate behavior. Reinforcement must be frequent and intense. (In other words, where the average child might be motivated to complete school tasks by the promise of a weekly sticker, children with ADHD tend to need larger and more frequent sources of motivation.) Long-term tasks need to be broken down into smaller, more manageable steps.

HELPFUL HINTS FOR PARENTS AND EDUCATORS

Many parents and educators have found ways to make life at home and school a better experience for children with ADHD.

A child with ADHD does better if she can break down a task into small steps.

At School

- Seat children with ADHD at the front of the class but away from such distractions as doors and windows.
- Allow ADHD students to sit near students who model good behavior and study skills.
- Vary the classroom routine by planning physical activities between times when they must sit at their desks.
- Make sure there are no unnecessary objects or materials on the desktop.
- Establish eye contact with the child before giving her instructions. Also explain that you are about to give instructions and that she needs to listen carefully.
- Instead of giving several instructions at once, give one at time, in the fewest words possible. It can help to have the student repeat your instruction and even to write it down.
- Provide frequent feedback to help the child understand whether or not he is on track.
- Schedule the most important activities during the times the child concentrates best.
- Provide opportunities to succeed; be sure to acknowledge and reward the student when appropriate. "ADHD children will work to attain something interesting that's within their grasp. Getting an A some time down the road is not their idea of a meaningful reward," writes Dr. Jacqueline Stordy.

At Home

- Establish incentives for good behavior. Be sure to make the consequences of misbehavior clear.
- Channel the child's energy into sports—preferably a sport where he stays in motion much of the time.

Text-Dependent Questions

1. What is included in an IEP?
2. How is an IEP created?
3. What are some other treatments that could benefit a child with ADHD?

- Use calming background music to help your child focus.
- When traveling, be sure to take along the books, tapes, and toys your child will need to be amused.
- Keep shopping trips and other errands brief. Be sure not to start out on these when your child is tired.
  (Adapted from *The LCP Solution*, by B. Jacqueline Stordy, Ph.D.)

Research Project

Children with ADHD will often receive special education. Use the Internet or talk to special education teachers in your school to find the answers to these questions:

- What education is required to be a special education teacher?
- What personal strengths do special education teachers need in order to do their jobs?
- What is hard about this job?
- What is rewarding about this job?
- Is this a career you would consider for yourself? Why or why not?

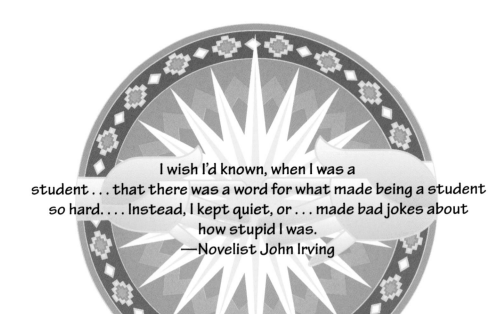

I wish I'd known, when I was a
student . . . that there was a word for what made being a student
so hard. . . . Instead, I kept quiet, or . . . made bad jokes about
how stupid I was.
—Novelist John Irving

8

HOPE

My class had a really good discussion about ADHD and other learning problems that afternoon. Mrs. Rose talked to us for quite a while about what ADHD meant, and I was surprised to hear how much she knew about it. Then she *really* surprised us by telling us that she'd had some of the same symptoms as Connor when she was growing up.

"Except, as is often the case with girls, I didn't have the hyperactivity part of the problem. So I didn't get into as many—shall we say, *interesting*—situations as Connor has," she said, smiling at me.

There was some laughter from kids in the class, but this time, it was friendly, if you know what I mean.

Then an amazing thing happened, even more amazing than having Mrs. Rose tell us she'd had ADHD. Jock talked in class. All by himself, without the teacher making him answer a question or anything.

He raised his hand and asked if he could say some things, and Mrs. Rose nodded. Then he told us how it felt to be out of control, the way he used to be, and how it felt now. "I'm not that way anymore," he said. "I take medicine that helps me control myself and pay attention better, the same as some of you do. But some of you won't let me change, so I just don't talk to you or try to make friends with you. But that doesn't mean I don't want to."

Mrs. Rose decided we should put away our country posters for a whole week and do a one-page paper on learning problems instead. We could pick any problem we wanted, but we had to find the name of a famous person who had had that problem and gone on to overcome it. I couldn't believe all the famous people who had this kind of stuff!

After that, things started changing, at least a little bit, in our class. I noticed that Jock started talking to people now and then, even to some of the girls. And the other sixth-graders seemed to treat me like I mattered more, now that I had stood up for Connor and spoken my mind.

Things were changing at home, too. My parents found out that Dr. Harmon wasn't entirely against using Ritalin or other medicines for ADHD. He had us all go to his office for a meeting so he could explain some things.

"To treat ADHD, you must use a *combination* of things," he said. "My worry is that, if parents put a child on medicine right up front, they may expect the medicine to take care of everything. They may not ever investigate other ways to deal with the problem.

"Some children with ADHD may only need changes in their environment, changes that give them the chance to learn new behavior patterns. Along with that, they may need a different diet, or any of the other things you've tried. Sometimes, those changes are enough. Sometimes, as with Connor, they're not. After you've tried other ways to help, then I say, if a child still needs medicine, give him medicine!

I'm glad to report that I survived sixth grade.

It even seems kind of funny to me now, how worried I was back then about being a "normal" sixth-grader and all. We're more grown up, now that I'm in seventh grade, so I don't worry so much about what other people think. I'm just working on being me.

Connor survived kindergarten, too. My parents put him on Ritalin, but they'd already made so many changes that, like I told you, he was starting to do better even before the medicine kicked in. He just needed the extra help that Ritalin gave him.

It's been a little strange at our house this past year. When Connor's taking the medicine, he's very calm and acts like other people. But for a while on weekends and longer breaks, he took "vacations" from the medicine. That's because my parents, especially my mom, worried that the Ritalin would affect his growth and stuff. But finally, after talking to some other doctors besides Dr. Harmon, my parents decided to keep Connor on his medicine all the time. He doesn't care at all about eating when he's taking it, which drives my mother to distraction, as she says, but now she spends a lot of time trying recipes she gets from other "ADHD mothers" on the Web—things that will give Connor the most nutrition possible, even if all he'll do is nibble.

Dad practices martial arts with Connor every night, and they've started building this huge model railroad layout in the basement. Dad says it's good for Connor's concentration, but I think the best thing for Connor is just spending all that extra time with Dad.

Kevin and Tim and I thought we'd get all our TVs back once Connor went on Ritalin. But Mom and Dad said the changes were permanent, and we'd get used to it. I was mad at first, but they were right. I did get used to it. In fact, I'd almost rather read together or play games than sit around watching TV like we used to—almost.

So, as you can probably imagine, I feel kind of bad about some of the stuff I said in the beginning of this journal, about how there should be a book called *The Ten Most Important Signs That You Have a Brother with ADHD, and What to Do About It.* Or maybe there *should* be a book like that. Maybe I'll even write it. I know so much about ADHD now that I'm thinking of going to medical school and becoming a pediatrician or some other kind of doctor who helps people with this problem. Like Dr. *Harmon.*

And if I do write that book, when I get to the end, I'll tell everybody the most important thing to do when you get a brother with ADHD. You just love him. Because chances are, he'll be a pretty special brother.

LEARNING STYLES

Not all intelligence can be measured by IQ tests; each child has a different way of learning.

In fact, according to Harvard researcher Howard Gardner, there are seven distinct intelligences, and Armstrong urges schools to include learning opportunities in each of the seven areas listed below. It is important to decide which learning areas each child is talented in and to encourage and support that talent.

Linguistic

This is the intelligence of words, and a child with a high linguistic intelligence will like to read, tell stories, and memorize facts.

Logical-Mathematical

This is the intelligence of reasoning, and children with a high level will like math and/or science, will easily handle number problems, brainteasers, and logic games and will be attracted to logical patterns.

Spatial

This is the intelligence of pictures and images, and the child who has a high level of it draws well, remembers visual details, thinks visually, and may be attracted to video games.

Bodily-Kinesthetic

This is the intelligence of physical skill, and children who have it like to work with their hands, enjoy athletics, and need to move in order to learn.

Musical

This is the intelligence of melody, tone, and rhythm. Children with musical intelligence enjoy listening to music and have a good sense of rhythm.

Interpersonal

This is the intelligence of getting along with others. A child with this intelligence has many friends, likes to socialize, shows empathy, and works well with others.

A student with ADHD may benefit from using computers or working one-on-one in the classroom.

Intrapersonal

This is the intelligence of self-knowledge, and children with it understand their own strengths and weaknesses, are self-confident, and reflect on their own experiences and learn from them.

COPING WITH DISABILITY

Sometimes, children and teenagers feel uncomfortable about taking a medication every day. They may feel that because they take medicine they are different from their classmates or that there's something seriously wrong with them. CH.A.D.D. (Children and Adults with Attention Deficit Disorders), a leading organization for people with attention disorders, suggests several ways that parents and teachers can help children view the medication in a positive way:

- Compare the pills to eyeglasses, braces, and allergy medications used by other children in their class. Explain that their medicine is simply a tool to help them focus and pay attention.
- Point out that they're lucky their problem can be helped. Encourage them to identify ways the medicine makes it easier to do things that are important to them, like make friends, succeed at school, and play.

Strategies for Teens and Adults with ADHD

- When necessary, ask the teacher or boss to repeat instructions rather than guess.
- Break large assignments or job tasks into small, simple tasks. Set a deadline for each task and reward yourself as you complete each one.
- Each day, make a list of what you need to do. Plan the best order for doing each task. Then make a schedule

for doing them. Use a calendar or daily planner to keep yourself on track.

- Work in a quiet area. Do one thing at a time. Give yourself short breaks.
- Write things you need to remember in a notebook with dividers. Write different kinds of information like assignments, appointments, and phone numbers in different sections. Keep the book with you all of the time.
- Post notes to help remind yourself of things you need to do. Tape notes on the bathroom mirror, on the refrigerator, in your school locker, or on the dashboard of your car—wherever you're likely to need the reminder.
- Store similar things together. For example, keep all your Nintendo disks in one place and tape cassettes in another. Keep canceled checks in one place and bills in another.

A student with ADHD may enjoy learning to play a musical instrument, so long as perfection is not required of her.

A child with ADHD may feel left out and discouraged. Adults with this disorder often experience some of the same feelings.

Research Project

This book states that ADHD can be a controversial topic. Go online to find out more about the various controversies connected with this condition. Pick one and list the arguments on each side of the issue.

- Create a routine. Get yourself ready for school or work at the same time, in the same way, every day.
- Exercise, eat a balanced diet, and get enough sleep.

Text-Dependent Questions

1. What has Shauna learned by the end of the book? How has she changed?
2. What kinds of intelligence do you think you have?

FURTHER READING

Gehret, J. *The Don't-Give-Up Kid: and Learning Disabilities.* Fairport, N.Y.: Verbal Images Press, 2009.

Haber, Julian Stuart. *The Great Misdiagnosis, ADHD.* Dallas: Taylor Trade, 2003.

Hallowell, E., and J. Ratey. *Driven to Distraction.* New York: Pantheon Books, 2011.

Kelly, K., and P. Ramundo. *You Mean I'm Not Lazy, Stupid, or Crazy?!* Cincinnati, Ohio: Tyrell and Jeremy Press, 2006.

Levine, Mel. *A Mind at a Time.* New York: Simon & Schuster, 2003.

Nadeau, K., and E. Dixon. *Learning to Slow Down and Pay Attention.* Annandale, Va.: Chesapeake Psychological Publications, 2004.

Weiss, L. *Attention Deficit Disorder in Adults.* Dallas: Taylor, 2005.

FOR MORE INFORMATION

ADD Anonymous
www.pel-anon.org/addanon

ADHD.com
www.adhd.com

The All Kinds of Minds Web site
www.allkindsofminds.org

CH.A.D.D. (Children and Adults with Attention Deficit Disorder)
www.chadd.org

Council for Exceptional Children
www.cec.sped.org

Federation of Families for Children's Mental Health
www.ffcmh.org

The Mental Health Net
adhd.mentalhelp.net

The National Attention Deficit Disorder Association
www.add.org

National Information Center for Children and Youth with Disabilities
    (NICHCY)
www.nichcy.org

National Resource Center on ADHD
www.help4adhd.org

The Substance Abuse and Mental Health Services Administration
www.samhsa.gov

Publisher's Note:

The websites listed on these pages were active at the time of publication. The publisher is not responsible for websites that have changed their address or discontinued operation since the date of publication. The publisher will review and update the websites upon each reprint.

SERIES GLOSSARY OF KEY TERMS

Accessibility: An environment that allows people with disabilities to participate as much as they can.

Accommodation: A change in how a student receives instruction, without substantially changing the instructional content.

Achievement test: A standardized test that measures a student's performance in academic areas such as math, reading, and writing.

Acting out: Behavior that's inappropriate within the setting.

Adaptive behavior: The extent to which an individual is able to adjust to and apply new skills to new environments, tasks, objects, and people.

Ambulatory: Able to walk independently.

American Sign Language (ASL): A language based on gestures that is used by people who are deaf in the United States and Canada.

Americans with Disabilities Act (ADA): In 1990, Congress passed this act, which provides people who have disabilities with the same freedoms as Americans who do not have disabilities. The law addresses access to buildings and programs, as well as housing and employment.

Anxiety: An emotional state of fear, often not attached to any direct threat, which can cause sweating, increased pulse, and breathing difficulty.

Aphasia: Loss of the ability to speak.

Articulation: The ability to express oneself through sounds, words, and sentences.

Asperger syndrome: An disorder that is on the autism spectrum, which can cause problems with nonverbal learning disorder and social interactions.

Assessment: The process of collecting information about a student's learning needs through tests, observations, and interviewing the student, the family, and others. Assistive technology: Any item or piece of equipment that is used to improve the capabilities of a child with a disability.

Attention-deficit/hyperactivity Disorder (ADHD): A disorder that can cause inappropriate behavior, including poor attention skills, impulsivity, and hyperactivity.

Autism spectrum disorder: A range of disabilities that affect verbal and nonverbal communication and social interactions.

Bipolar disorder: A brain disorder that causes uncontrollable changes in moods, behaviors, thoughts, and activities.

Blind (legally): Visual acuity for distance vision of 20/200 or less in the better eye after best correction with conventional lenses; or a visual field of no greater than 20 degrees in the better eye.

Bullying: When a child faces threats, intimidation, name-calling, gossip, or physical violence.

Cerebral palsy (CP): Motor impairment caused by brain damage during birth or before birth. It can be mild to severe, does not get worse, and cannot be cured. Chronic: A condition that persists over a long period of time.

Cognitive: Having to do with remembering, reasoning, understanding, and using judgment.

Congenital: Any condition that is present at birth.

Counseling: Advice or help through talking, given by someone qualified to give such help.

Deaf: A hearing loss so severe that speech cannot be understood, even with a hearing aid, even if some sounds may still be perceived.

Developmental: Having to do with the steps or stages in growth and development of a child.

Disability: A limitation that interferes with a person's ability to walk, hear, talk, or learn.

Down syndrome: An abnormal chromosomal condition that changes the development of the body and brain, often causing intellectual disabilities.

Early intervention: Services provided to infants and toddlers ages birth to three who are at risk for or are showing signs of having a slower than usual development.

Emotional disturbance (ED): An educational term (rather than psychological) where a student's inability to build or maintain satisfactory interpersonal relationships with peers and teachers, inappropriate types of behavior or feelings, and moods of unhappiness or depression get in the way of the student being able to learn and function in a school setting.

Epilepsy: A brain disorder where the electrical signals in the brain are disrupted, causing seizures. Seizures can cause brief changes in a person's body movements, awareness, emotions, and senses (such as taste, smell, vision, or hearing).

Fine motor skills: Control of small muscles in the hands and fingers, which are needed for activities such as writing and cutting.

Gross motor skills: Control of large muscles in the arms, legs, and torso, which are needed for activities such as running and walking.

Hard-of-hearing: A hearing loss that may affect the student's educational performance.

Heredity: Traits acquired from parents.

Individualized Education Plan (IEP): A written education plan for students ages 5 to 22 with disabilities, developed by a team of professionals, (teachers, therapists, etc.) and the child's parent(s), which is reviewed and updated yearly. It contains a description of the child's level of development, learning needs, goals and objectives, and services the child will receive.

Individuals with Disabilities Education Act (IDEA): The Individuals with Disabilities Education Act (IDEA) is the nation's federal special education law that requires public schools to serve the educational needs of students with disabilities. IDEA requires that schools provide special education services to eligible students as outlined in a student's IEP, and it also provides very specific requirements to guarantee a free appropriate education for students with disabilities in the least restrictive environment.

Intervention: A planned activity to increase students' skills.

Learning disability: A general term for specific kinds of learning problems that can cause a person to have challenges learning and using certain skills, such as reading, writing, listening, speaking, reasoning, and doing math.

Least restrictive environment: The educational setting or program that provides a student with as much contact as possible with children without disabilities, while still appropriately meeting all of the child's learning and physical needs.

Mainstreaming: Providing any services, including education, for children with disabilities, in a setting with other children who do not have disabilities.

Motor: Having to do with muscular activity.

Nonambulatory: Not able to walk independently.

Occupational therapist (OT): A professional who helps individuals be able to handle meaningful activities of daily life such as self-care skills, education, recreation, work or social interaction.

Palate: The roof of the mouth.

Paraplegia: Paralysis of the legs and lower part of the body.

Partially sighted: A term formally used to indicate visual acuity of 20/70 to 20/200, but also used to describe visual impairment in which usable vision is present.

Pediatrics: The medical treatment of children.

Physical therapist (PT): A person who helps individuals improve the use of bones, muscles, joints, and/or nerves.

Prenatal: Existing or occurring prior to birth.

Quadriplegia: Paralysis affecting all four limbs.

Referral: In special education, students are referred for screening and evaluation to see if they are eligible for special education services.

Self-care skills: The ability to care for oneself; usually refers to basic habits of dressing, eating, etc.

Special Education: Specialized instruction made to fit the unique learning strengths and needs of each student with disabilities in the least restrictive environment.

Speech impaired: Communication disorder such as stuttering, impaired articulation, a language impairment, or a voice impairment, which adversely affects a child's educational performance.

Speech pathologist: A trained therapist, who provides treatment to help a person develop or improve articulation, communication skills, and oral-motor skills.

Spina bifida: A problem that happens in the first month of pregnancy when the spinal column doesn't close completely.

Standardized tests: Tests that use consistent directions, procedures, and criteria for scoring, which are often administered to many students in many schools across the country.

Stereotyping: A generalization in which individuals are falsely assigned traits they do not possess based on race, ethnicity, religion, disability, or gender.

Symptom: An observable sign of an illness or disorder.

Syndrome: A set of symptoms that occur together.

Therapy: The treatment or application of different techniques to improve specific conditions for curing or helping to live with various disorders.

Traumatic Brain Injury (TBI): Physical damage to the brain that could result in physical, behavioral, or mental changes depending on which area of the brain is injured.

Visually impaired: Any degree of vision loss that affects an individual's ability to perform the tasks of daily life, which is caused by a visual system that is not working properly or not formed correctly.

Vocational education: Educational programs that prepare students for paid or unpaid employment, or which provide additional preparation for a career that doesn't require a college degree.

INDEX

ABOUT THE AUTHOR
AND THE CONSULTANTS

Shirley Brinkerhoff was a writer, editor, speaker, and musician. She graduated from Cornerstone University with a Bachelor of Music degree, and from Western Michigan University with a Master of Music degree. She wrote six young adult novels, thirteen informational books, and scores of short stories and articles.

Dr. Lisa Albers is a developmental behavioral pediatrician at Children's Hospital Boston and Harvard Medical School, where her responsibilities include outpatient pediatric teaching and patient care in the Developmental Medicine Center. She currently is Director of the Adoption Program, Director of Fellowships in Developmental and Behavioral Pediatrics, and collaborates in a consultation program for community health centers. She is also the school consultant for the Walker School, a residential school for children in the state foster care system.

Dr. Carolyn Bridgemohan is an instructor in pediatrics at Harvard Medical School and is a board-certified developmental behavioral pediatrician on staff in the Developmental Medicine Center at Children's Hospital, Boston. Her clinical practice includes children and youth with autism, hearing impairment, developmental language disorders, global delays, mental retardation, and attention and learning disorders. Dr. Bridgemohan is coeditor of *Bright Futures Case Studies for Primary Care Clinicians: Child Development and Behavior*, a curriculum used nationwide in pediatric residency training programs.

Cindy Croft is the State Special Needs Director in Minnesota, coordinating Project EXCEPTIONAL MN, through Concordia University. Project EXCEPTIONAL MN is a state project that supports the inclusion of children in community settings through training, on-site consultation, and professional development. She also teaches as adjunct faculty for Concordia University, St. Paul, Minnesota. She has worked in the special needs arena for the past fifteen years.

Dr. Laurie Glader is a developmental pediatrician at Children's Hospital in Boston where she directs the Cerebral Palsy Program and is a staff pediatrician with the Coordinated Care Services, a program designed to meet the needs of children with special health care needs. Dr. Glader also teaches regularly at Harvard Medical School. Her work with public agencies includes New England SERVE, an organization that builds connections between state health departments, health care organizations, community providers, and families. She is also the staff physician at the Cotting School, a school specializing in the education of children with a wide range of special health care needs.